Calais and its Border Politics

T0353041

Calais has a long history of transient refugee settlements and is often narrated through the endeavour to 'sanitize' it by both the English and the French in their policy and media discourses. *Calais and its Border Politics* encapsulates the border politics of Calais as an entry port through the refugee settlements known as the 'Jungle'. By deconstructing how the jungle is a constant threat to the civilization and sanity of Calais, the book traces the story of the jungle, both its revival and destruction as a recurrent narrative through the context of border politics. The book approaches Calais historically and through the key concept of the camp or the 'jungle' – a metaphor that becomes crucial to the inhuman approach to the settlement and in the justifications to destroy it continuously. The demolition and rebuilding of Calais also emphasizes the denigration of humanity in the border sites.

The authors offer a comprehensive insight into the making and unmaking of one of Europe's long-standing refugee camps. The book explores the history of refugee camps in Calais and provides an insight into its representation and governance over time. The book provides an interdisciplinary perspective, employing concepts of space making, human form and corporeality, as well as modes of representation of the 'Other' to narrate the story of Calais as a border space through time, up to its recent representations in the media.

This book's exploration of the representation and governance of the contentious Calais camps will be an invaluable resource to students and scholars of forced migration, border politics, displacement, refugee crisis, camps and human trauma.

Yasmin Ibrahim is a Reader in Communications at Queen Mary, University of London, UK.

Anita Howarth is a Senior Lecturer in Journalism, Brunel University, UK.

Routledge Research on the Global Politics of Migration

Calais and its Border Politics

From Control to Demolition

Yasmin Ibrahim and Anita Howarth

Routledge
Taylor & Francis Group

LONDON AND NEW YORK

First published 2018
by Routledge

First published 2017
by Routledge

2 Park Square, Milton Park, Abingdon, Oxfordshire OX14 4RN
52 Vanderbilt Avenue, New York, NY 10017

Routledge is an imprint of the Taylor & Francis Group, an informa business

First issued in paperback 2019

British Library Cataloguing-in-Publication Data
A catalogue record for this book is available from the British Library

Library of Congress Cataloging-in-Publication Data
A catalog record has been requested for this book

ISBN: 978-1-138-04916-1 (hbk)
ISBN: 978-0-367-82099-2 (pbk)

Typeset in Times New Roman
by Swales & Willis Ltd. Exeter, Devon, UK

To all the displaced children. To lost innocence. To lost childhood. To lost lives.

Contents

Illustrations

Figures

Table

Preface

It was the tears of the children that drew us to Calais. It was a line in the newspapers about another grand demolition of the Jungle in Calais in 2009. A circus act had been concocted to impress the public that the authorities on both sides were indeed in charge. It described with detail the bulldozers and flame throwers. Amidst all that noise were these tiny figures in tears. There were no images of them. Just a line that captured their desolation. Their loss. Over the years, Calais will remain a contentious issue making headlines and making enemies of neighbours, further fragmenting the united front of the EU. The jungles belonged to nobody but they were a curse. The unwanted in Europe is a story of moral panic. A story of threat and extreme unease, particularly at election periods. The invisible children alluded to in the earlier articles will become real images in media coverage. We will see them dangled on razor wires, perhaps even a grave at the camp site. While the hidden and invisible became realms of new found curiosity in media coverage, Calais remains a cartography of human violence. Episodes and episodes of human drama and desperation and equally annihilation of makeshift quarters will happen with a frenzy to cleanse and sanitize Calais and to return it to normalcy. Calais as overrun by the Jungle and filled with human squalor and filth will be contrasted with stories of Jungle residents having modern toilets and a library with children's book. Stories of futility will be mediated by volunteer kitchens and charity groups offering human help on the ground. Canned food and makeshift churches providing a glimmer of hope. A sliver of salvation.

The reclaiming of Calais will play out in numerous tunes and they will take more atavistic forms over time. The denial of human rights along with basic human amenities will unleash a politics of depletion; where there will be a defacing of the 'human' in the humanitarian project. The denigration of the human form and the animalistic renditions that ensue is about a mirror to humanity, another chapter in the violent history of migration in Europe. Another story of human displacement that has yet to find its happy ending.

The UK's response to this crises has been confused and fragmented, often overplaying security issues at the expense of the beleaguered human form. Theresa May's (then home secretary prior to her premiership) response was to send more razor wire to shore up the defences at the border. The razor wire in fact is symbolic of the crisis in Calais. It became the very object that residents of Calais hope to cross and over time these form a relationship with the refugee body, where cuts, gaping wounds and gangrene infections reveal their attempts to cross into Britain. Attempts at redemption. Attempts to be not reduced to 'bare life'. Others are reduced to fatal statistics in their quest to escape the madness of the camp. While others languish in detention centres, where both daylight and hope arrive in scant measure.

1   Calais in constant crossroads

Introduction

This book is about the constant eruptions produced by the so-called 'migrant' crisis at the Anglo-French borders of Calais. It's about the stories of Jungles that sprout in the White suburbia. Jungles that seem to be virulent in reducing carefully planned suburbs into swamp lands. Order into chaos. The sort of turbulence that warrants armed intervention and demolition. These refugee camps labelled the Jungle are wholly inconvenient for they turn neighbouring states into turf wars with blazing accusations of the other not being resolute in attending to the 'migrant' problem. These constant skirmishes, name calling and cries of irresponsibility are part of the 'madness' that the Jungle produces, beyond the madness the Jungle inflicts on its own inhabitants. The constant resurgence of the Jungle and the quest to make these makeshift settlements disappear become recurring tropes in the modern and contemporary history of Calais, invoking a spiral of violence on the Other and against the Other.

The 20-mile stretch between Calais and Dover is the narrowest point in the English Channel between Great Britain and the European mainland. Calais–Dover has practical significance as a major route in and out of Britain for people and goods (Readman, 2014). With the opening of the Channel Tunnel in 1994 Calais became the major transit hub with migrants congregating there in the hope that they could hide on trucks heading across to Britain to break through border controls. The imposing of juxtaposed controls[1] means that Calais is variously represented as a 'bottleneck, barrier, border and breakthrough point' (McNeil, 2014; Figure 1.1).

The movement of the refugees in Calais and their treatment reflects Britain's reticent attitude to EU migrant and asylum policies where it has been neither 'wholly in or wholly out', signing up to a little over half of the measures introduced by the EU such that engagement has been 'conditional and differential' (Geddes, 2005, p. 732) with a particular emphasis on security

Figure 1.1 TGV TMST n° 3011/2 at the exit of the Channel Tunnel at Coquelles, French side, 2014

Source: Billy69150. © BY-SA 4.0 International license.

and border controls at the external frontiers of Britain. In July 2002, the UK and France reached an agreement to close the Sangatte refugee camp as it was attracting migrants and had become a constant source of contention between the two countries. With the closure of Sangatte, asylum seekers and migrants in Calais assumed a relatively low profile. However, growing numbers fleeing conflict and persecution in Iraq, Somalia and Afghanistan set up informal camps known as 'the Jungle' which attracted media attention in 2009, as did the subsequent demolition of the camps. The Calais crisis came back into media scrutiny due to bigger events in the Mediterranean, where unprecedented numbers of refugees were risking their lives in over-crowded and rickety boats. On 2 September 2015, the tragic image of Alan Kurdi dead on the beach ignited further interest in the refugee and humanitarian crisis leading to a surge in photo coverage of both the Mediterranean and Calais crisis. The forced migration in Syria and parts of Africa converged with anxieties about opening up the UK to new members such as Romania and Bulgaria between 2010 and 2016.

The irregular migration into the EU during the Balkans conflagration in the late 1990s was a precursor of what was to come two decades later. In 2014 political instability around the world escalated, prompting the UN High Commissioner for Refugees to warn that the world was facing its biggest 'forced migration crisis' since the Second World War (Gower and Smith, 2015). The scale of displacement has required more coordination between states than before (Papademetriou, 2015). Ongoing instability across its borders with the Middle East and North Africa as well as sub-Saharan Africa and Afghanistan have contributed to Europe's 'migrant crisis' reaching a crescendo in 2015. The crisis had been building since the 'Arab Spring' in 2011, but in 2015 Frontex estimated that twice as many asylum seekers and migrants, or some 859,000 people, had arrived on Greek and Italian shores in the first 11 months of the year as in the previous five years combined, culminating in 4,000 arrivals a day at one point on the Greek islands with 3695 dead or missing while crossing the Mediterranean in 2015 (cf. Papademetriou, 2015).

Contemporary refugee crisis: Calais and its significance

The crisis in Calais and the Mediterranean became a testing ground for the UK in terms of its humanitarian response, particularly the provision of sanctuary. In the case of Calais, it became a long running battle with the French with both sides claiming each other's inadequacy in managing the crisis. The constant sprouting of refugee camps in Calais and the invocation to act by both charities and alt-right anti-immigrant groups on the growing numbers in Calais demonstrated a Britain wary of people sneaking into its borders. The inhabitants of the camps were often portrayed by ministers and right-wing media as economic opportunists seeking to take advantage of the welfare system in the UK (Howarth and Ibrahim, 2012). Equally, shipwrecks in the Mediterranean were seen as people being trafficked or being irresponsible in taking huge risks to cross the seas through unsafe passage where there was the risk of drowning. The response to the Mediterranean demonstrated Britain's existing arrangement to externalize border controls, manage the influx and process the applications. It outsourced these to third or other European countries such as Turkey and Greece and vetted refugees in the UN camps in Syria rather than in Europe. The slippage in discourse between the refugee and the migrant also meant that the 'displaced' were often pressed through the lens of the 'suspect body' where the humanitarianism ideal could be suspended or denied.

In contrast to the crisis in the Mediterranean, Calais has always been a point of contention between the British and the French. By the late 1990s, it had attracted growing political, public and media attention as rising numbers of migrants and refugees fleeing from the Balkan Wars and conflict in Afghanistan and Iraq congregated (Geddes, 2005; Rygiel, 2011). In 1999, the French government, concerned by the visible signs of humanitarian distress in which thousands of refugees, including pregnant women and children, were forced to sleep on the streets and in the parks of Calais and neighbouring towns, asked the Red Cross to open a refugee camp in Sangatte, a giant warehouse half a mile from the entrance to the Tunnel (Fassin, 2012). Originally intended to house 600 people, by 2002 over 2000 people were seeking nightly shelter in increasing squalor as the Red Cross struggled to manage overcrowding. By 2002, companies had spent millions shoring up defences around key railway stations, the Eurotunnel and the port and on greater running costs of more security guards.[2] The companies began to lobby both governments to close Sangatte, claiming that it had become a magnet for illegal migrants. Only after they had taken their campaign to the media and rumours had begun to circulate that Al-Qaeda had infiltrated Sangatte and posed an imminent security threat did the French and British governments agree to close the shelter (Hills, 2002). The interweaving of a security threat with a humanitarian crisis in Calais demarcated the notion of refuge as a symbol of danger and a fault line in British immigration policies. Calais became the 'frontline' in the fight against migration (Keyes, 2004) and in securing Britain from an 'invasion' of migrants.

Between 2002 and 2015, the French authorities allowed humanitarian relief in the form of basic medical care, food and blankets to be provided by local charities, Doctors of the World and the Catholic Church. It nevertheless imposed a de facto ban on any semi-permanent shelters in Calais on the grounds that it attracted illegal migrants. The migrants and refugees, out of necessity, set up informal shelters and tents that gradually grew into sprawling camps, labelled the 'Jungle' and that were periodically demolished by the French authorities, often citing 'humanitarian' reasons. Notably, the British and French governments have consistently labelled this transient population at Calais as 'illegal migrants' rather than refugees to avoid having to provide for them or to process requests for asylum. The acute nature of the situation resulted in the UN opening its first-ever office to deal with the humanitarian crisis of forced displacement in 2009.

Britain has over time focused on securing the border at Calais and the Channel Tunnel where an estimated 1 per cent of all the refugees in the EU had congregated. It prompted the government to announce it would enhance security at the access points to the Channel Tunnel by spending millions of pounds (Hall and Allen, 2015) including the installation of razor wire around the access points to the Channel Tunnel and the roads leading to it. The UK's hard-line response underscored the need to assuage hostile anti-immigration attitudes in Britain. Calais is a repository of a long convoluted history of entanglement with passage, invasion, closure and border control.

Calais has a long history of creating refugees through expulsion and as a gateway for those seeking sanctuary in Britain. Calais is about footprints – ancient and recent, guarded and transient. It's been traversed and crossed over by the desperate and the routine. Filled with hope and tarnished through violence – it speaks of the conflicted and unsettled nature of the border and border tensions. Tensions that never resolve yet are constantly pulled into the spotlight by bodies that are expiated from its guarded boundary. It speaks of new forms of vigilance and sordid discoveries of cold immobile bodies concealed in container vehicles; frozen with desire for new life yet inscribed through their flight in defying the futility of their label as the economically dispossessed. Seen as opportunistic bodies that will impregnate and leach the benefit system of the UK, Calais throws up a body politic of the 'unwanted'.

This book is an attempt to assemble and disassemble Calais through the lens of the Jungle. These refugee camps dubbed the Jungle in everyday discourse and media terminology are symbolic of the enormity of the refugee crisis that Europe faces today. The metaphor of the Jungle is emblematic. It captures the 'opportunistic migrant' through a discourse of reductionism. Reduction into the animalistic. Reduction into the uncouth. Reduction into the inhumane. The Jungle is not one you cultivate, for it has the potential to grow and take over. The association of the 'migrant' with the untamed Jungle is not incidental but becomes ideologically and instrumentally vital in rationalising its decimation. This book is an attempt to look into the Jungle and relocate its humanity. It is an attempt to relocate the human in the border politics of depletion. And death.

Calais and its situated geography

The politics of the Anglo-French borderlands have been shaped over centuries by its cartography. Positioned at the narrowest point of the English Channel and emerging as a natural crossing point of the sea barrier, the geo-location of Calais is both about its natural defence against invasion (i.e. surrounded by sea) and mobility as a route for passage. Its dual renderings of defence and mobility are captured by William Shakespeare's John of Gaunt who says of Britain:

> This fortress built by Nature for herself
> Against infection and the hand of war . . .
> This precious stone set in the silver sea
> Which serves in the office of a wall
> Or as a moat defensive to a house
> Against the envy of less happier lands.
>
> (Shakespeare, 1993, 2: 1)

The dominant and foremost notion of the Channel as a 'moat defensive' has been constantly invoked through time. From the sinking of the Spanish

Armada in 1588 to Hitler's aborted plans to invade, a leitmotif of Calais emerges. This sense of the UK as an Island nation and its insularity located through its geography is a key part of the British imaginary and in tandem there has been resistance to acknowledging Calais as the end of a tunnel on the sea-bed that would inextricably link the UK spatially with the rest of the continent into an European bloc for more than a century (Darian-Smith, 1999). Even since the opening of Eurotunnel in May 1994, Britain has remained deeply conflicted and tightly welded to the neoliberal commitment to trade yet wary of anything that might compromise or be seen by the public to compromise defence and sovereignty through closer links with Europe.

The Channel has also, since the Middle Ages, been imagined as a 'roadway' and Calais as a 'gateway' to Europe crystallized in the capture of the town by Edward III in 1347 with the intention of using it as a point for disembarkation for future invasions (Wallace, 2008; Lambert 2011, p. 245). The Kingdom of England held Calais till 1558 when the French recaptured the town and the loss of their gateway to France prompted the English retreat across the Channel. The English turned inwards reconstructing nationhood around the insularity and exceptionalism of an island nation, and outward beyond Europe to the sea lanes and maritime empire that later supported colonisation (Wallace, 2008; Readman, 2014). In the social imaginary of Englishmen such as William Hogarth, Calais became a place 'where the English (where England) used to be' and 'where the foreign begins' (Wallace, 2008, p. 2) or as popularized by British MP George Wigg in 1949, it was 'where the wog begins' (Wigg, 1949); 'wog' being an offensive racial slur.

The retreat in 1558 nevertheless was not total. After the Napoleonic wars, lace workers from Nottingham set up businesses in Calais so they could sell directly to the lucrative European market for luxury goods and bypass English customs duties on exports. Their survival and sustenance unfortunately proved precarious after the 1848 revolution with the surge of French nationalism and, unable to return to Britain during recession, many of the workers fled to the colonies, in particular Australia (Bensimon, 2016; Alderman, 2017).[3]

The oppositional notions of 'moat defensive' and 'gateway' were again cast into sharp relief during the conflicts of the twentieth century. In the First World War, the ports of Calais and Dunkirk facilitated the offloading of men and munitions from Britain for the frontline, with much of the work undertaken by Chinese, Egyptians, Indians and South Africans brought in from the colonies as cheap labour to free up British soldiers for fighting (Griffin, 1976).[4] Calais remained a source of anxiety in the Second World War with the German High Command fearing invasion near the port. After the Second World War and with the loss of empire, Britain turned back to Europe for trade and sought reintegration with the emerging economic trading block of Western Europe. Twenty years after the erection of the Atlantic Wall, the politics of Europe had shifted from conflict to cooperation, Britain having lost its colonies was keen on cultivating new markets and placed its priority on minimising the barriers to crossing. A channel tunnel connecting Calais and Folkestone at this juncture was crafted as a symbol of cooperation and interconnectedness, seeking to negate the natural barrier of the sea. Since the opening of the Eurotunnel, Calais has become one of the busiest transit hubs in the world (see Schuster, 2003). Nord-Pas-de-Calais has over time been adversely affected by globalization, the collapse of the lace industry as well as the rise of National Front and resurgence of xenophobia particularly with its reinvention as a commercial transit hub (Sparks, 2015; Alderman, 2017).

A historicized spatiality: the figure of the refugee in Calais

In Calais, the refugee is a deeply-rooted historical figure dating from premodern times. Not only has Calais been a gateway to sanctuary in England (or vice versa), it has also been a space in which the refugee has been created through periodic expulsions since the 14th century. King Edward III having captured the town in 1347 adopted a policy of colonization and repopulation or 'deracination' in which existing residents were expelled, 'uncontaminated Englishness', or 'purs Engles' brought in (Wallace, 2008, p. 39) and for six generations Calais was an 'English town' in France (Rose, 2008). The French retook Calais in 1558 and, in a precursor of the later purge of Protestants, expelled the Huguenots who had worked for the English draining ditches and marshes. The purge after Protestantism was declared illegal in 1685, created England's first 'modern' refugees (Gwynn, 1985; Hintermaier, 2000) and the term réfugié meaning 'to take shelter, protect' entered into the English language as refugee in the 1680s was used to specifically refer to the Huguenots. It was not until the First World War that the term expanded in scope to mean 'one fleeing' (Online Etymology Dictionary).

During the eighteenth and nineteenth centuries Calais continued to be imagined and used as a gateway to sanctuary in Britain particularly during the wave of revolutions, nationalism and xenophobia that periodically convulsed Europe.[5] Refugees particularly in the Victorian era were attracted by a popular imaginary of Britain as a space of religious and political toleration where public opinion would not countenance the extradition of those who had sought refuge (Shaw, 2015). This began to change with the first mass refugee movement of the modern era in the flight of the Ashkenazi Jews from the Russian programmes of the 1880s through the seaports on the west coast of Europe including Calais. The exodus of the Ashkenazi Jews was a precursor of the mass displacement that was to reshape the European politics of the twentieth century. The Jews who arrived in Britain were met with an escalating anti-Semitism that culminated in the 1905 Aliens Act that not only reinstated border controls after a hiatus of 80 years, but also for the first time introduced asylum as a legal concept and distinguished the 'unwanted' refugee in the destitute, the diseased or the criminal (Bashford and McAdam, 2014).

The twentieth century has been defined by two interweaving but distinct phenomena that have prompted historians to call it the 'century of refugees' in which forced displacement reached unprecedented levels (Marrus, 1985). Zygmunt Bauman (1995) terms it the 'the age of the camp' where these spatial formations were not only unimaginable in their dehumanizing qualities and cruelty but also became the organizing and structuring principles of society.

Michael Marrus (1985) conceptualizes the 'century of refugees' in terms of the unprecedented scale of forced displacement that started with the First World War when forced displacement reached a hitherto unprecedented scale and even greater levels with the Second World War when civilians became the targets of warring armies (Panikos, 2011).[6] The 'century of refugees' was not only about large scale refugee movements but also the struggle of recipient states to cope with it, adding a new dynamic to international border politics and inter-state tensions. During the course of the century the concept of refugee became codified and expanded in international treaties that attempted to institutionalize the Kantian moral imperative of cosmopolitan law to offer hospitality to those fleeing persecution and conflict (see Kleingeld, 1998). Regardless of these broader shifts in moral sentiment, states have continued to respond with 'apathy and antipathy' towards the 'huge refugee inundations', the 'unwanted' of the twentieth century (Marrus, 1985). Notwithstanding the ideals encapsulated in international treaties, the refugee in the twentieth century came to be seen as a 'liminal figure who threatened social stability' in new ways (Gatrell, 2014, p. 2). In the First World War, the refugee could not readily be situated within the class structure (Gatrell, 2014, p. 8) and in the Second World War Britain and other European countries demonstrated a resistance to refugees through the figure of the Jewish refugee (London, 2000). During the Balkans conflict and the aftermath of the Arab Spring the resistance has been towards Muslims.

The notion of the twentieth century as the 'age of the camp' refers not only to their proliferation but also to the way in which the nation state and society in Nazi Germany and the Soviet Union were organized and structured around an 'archipelago of camps' intended to control mobility and govern life through coercion and violence (see Bauman, 1995; Minca, 2015; Stone, 2017). The political geographer Claudio Minca (2015) has drawn chilling cartographic links between the proliferation of the camps of the Nazi and Soviet eras and the contemporary network of detention centres that structure and organize asylum across Europe. Minca has suggested that the twenty-first century thus far is one when the camp as a 'spatial political technology' is found everywhere and 'camp thinking' has assumed new pervasive forms in politics and culture (Minca, 2015, p. 76).

Beyond refugee camps, Nord-Pas-de-Calais shares a connection with labour camps. In a grim foretaste of what was to come later, 17 camps housed nearly 140,000 of the Chinese Labour Corps in Northern France during the First World War, an estimated 20,000 of whom died from enemy attacks, disease and exhaustion but their contribution to the war effort was marginalized and all but erased until the turn of the millennium (Kennedy, 2014).[7] Between 1942 and 1944, there were 15 permanent and temporary camps in the prefecture housing forced labour used to construct the Atlantic Wall (Roberts, 2010). The camps included not only Belgian Jews (the ones from Calais having been deported to Auschwitz) but also prisoners of war and press ganged Russian labour including children as young as 12 years old and Spanish Republicans. Many of the slave labourers in the camps died within three months from beatings, hunger or harsh working conditions.

Calais as a palimpsest of routes and passage is evident south of Calais where there are the remnants of the concrete 'Jews Road' built along with the Atlantic Wall by forced labour in 1942 (see Roberts, 2010). The Wall stretched from Norway to Spain but some of its strongest fortifications were in Nord-Pas-de-Calais, the narrowest part of the English Channel where the German High Command expected the Allied attack to come. The labour camps that housed the Belgian Jews and conscripted labour that built the defences have long since gone but their footprints embedded in the concrete are still visible in the remnants of the road they built. The outputs of their labour, the 'architectural relics' of blockhouses, bunkers and bits of the original razor wire lie half submerged in dunes and the sea (Vanfleteren, 2014).

The erasure of the Chinese contribution, the concrete footprints and wartime relics are visible reminders of unimaginable brutality and the dehumanizing of the racialized Other. The context and the nature of the camps are too dissimilar to those of the Jungle but the trauma of the displaced Other and their incarceration through inhumane conditions forms an inextricable connection between the past and present, binding Calais into a repository of human suffering. Not only are the landscapes of Nord-Pas-de-Calais imbued with 'ghostly' reminders (Vanfleteren, 2014) but the temporal frames of the past and present co-mingle through a materiality where migrants expelled from demolished Jungles create makeshift shelters in the bunkers and blockhouse remnants of the wall from the past (Allen, 2009). The coalescing of the past and present also resonate in political discourse and popular culture.

Political and media discourses of successive Jungles in Calais have implicitly evoked history, some centuries old, in accounts of 'illegal migrants' laying 'siege' to Calais (Bracchi, 2009; Thornhill, 2014), 'breaching' the security of the Eurotunnel (*Guardian*, 2002; *The Times*, 2015) or the 'fortress Calais' surrounded by razor wire fencing (Stothard, 2015). A more explicit evoking of the past has come from Britain's Jewish community, some of whom were rescued from the extermination camps of Nazi Germany, in their call for a 'kindertransport' type scheme to save the unaccompanied children in the Jungle before it was demolished in October 2016 (Janner-Klausner, 2015). The UN equally evoked the past in cautioning Europe that it faced its biggest refugee crisis since the end of the Second World War; its criticisms of the inhumane conditions in the Jungles of Calais as an 'indictment' on society and Britain's response to the current crisis as a 'failure of leadership' implied that neither country had learned from the past. It reiterated how history had failed to educate humanity on the depth of its moral depravity.

Calais and the transient

Calais as a multi-modal transport hub has renewed its appeal as a gateway on the refugee trails for those keen to seek asylum in Britain. While Britain has embraced the neoliberal benefits of enhanced trade with Europe, it has remained profoundly fearful of ceding sovereignty to EU bureaucrats and distrustful of the willingness of its European neighbours to adequately police the external borders of the Union. This distrust was bolstered through time as British public and political sentiment hardened against immigration more generally (Ibrahim and Howarth, 2016). Fear and distrust coalesced into the UK opting out of the Schengen Agreement on free movement within the EU in order to retain its sovereign power to determine who may or may not enter its territory. The French seaboard, already the border between the continent and Britain, became the border between free movement and the reinstatement of hard controls, which were moved back to Calais after the opening of Eurotunnel. Large-scale incursions into the tunnel and onto the roads leading to the port prompted increasing securitization and Calais became a bottleneck for refugees and migrants whose presence in and around the border ebbed and flowed, depending on the conflict and oppression in states beyond the borders of the EU. Unable to return to their country of origin for fear of persecution and war, feeling unwanted in France yet obstructed from moving on by border controls, the refugees and migrants became trapped in growing numbers in the liminal spaces of the Calais Jungle.

Sixty years after the post-war crisis the refugee in Calais has become an abject figure, largely abandoned by both the UK and France. Beyond the odd token of 'humanitarianism', the precarity of the migrants is visibly demonstrated through the periodic demolition of informal camps, acts of erasure that serve as potent political tools to impress the unlimited power of the sovereign states. All that remains of the 2016 demolition of the Jungle are fragmented bits of barbed wire, broken bottles and a warning sign to 'keep out' (McGuinness, 2017). Despite the brutal demolitions, Calais is constantly inscribed with the figure of the refugee as they return at a rate of about a 100 a week. With no Jungle to return to they are forming 'secret' camps away from the gaze of the police while they continue their attempts to cross into Britain (Sheldrick, 2017). Away from the monitoring gaze of volunteers and aid groups in and near the camps, refugees and in particular unaccompanied children are vulnerable to attacks from fascist or alt-right groups and 'endemic police brutality' (Bulman, 2017b).

Today's refugees, the racialized 'other' from the former colonies, are highly visible and vulnerable as targets for the police and right-wing groups. The assumed insularity and isolation evoked in Shakespeare's moat defensive seems 'archaic' in an age of globalization where the 'carriers of infection and invasion are no longer the French – or, for that matter, the Jews, but instead refugees from failed states that France and Britain had a hand in creating' (Zaretsky, 2015).

The media have tapped into these historically rooted and latent fears in their accounts of 'migrants' using Sangatte or the Jungles as launch pads to cross the Channel, as 'incursions' onto trucks or 'migrant invasion' of the tunnel where its defences are repeatedly 'breached' (Boswell, 2012; Campbell *et al.*, 2015; Powley and Stacey, 2015; Robinson, 2016). The history and context of Calais becomes intertextual today as the medieval defence tactic of constructing a moat against these 'invaders' or 'marauders' is invoked through the erection of razor wire fencing and walls around the entrance of Eurotunnel to prevent stowaways heading across the Channel.

The refugee in Calais, as with many gateway or frontier towns, is a common but marginalized figure whose precarity was captured in Hogarth's 1748 painting, *The Gate of Calais* (Figure 1.2).[8] The Franco-phobe painting lampooned the decadence of the French clergy vis-à-vis the impoverished French soldiers but also captures the figure of a Jacobite refugee slumped in

Figure 1.2 O the Roast Beef of Old England (The Gate of Calais) by William
Hogarth and Charles Mosley, 1749

Source: © By-NC-NC (3.0 unported). Photo © Tate.

the shadows too exhausted to eat the onion next to him, the only food available to him (Davidson, 2000).

The pathos of today's refugees have been powerfully captured in four
paintings by the graffiti artist Banksy. One outside the French embassy in
London[9] is highly critical of police tactics in the Jungle camp and depicts a
young girl from the musical *Les Misérables* with tears in her eyes as CS gas
billowed towards her. The interactive work included a QR code beneath and
if viewers held their phone over the code it linked them to an online video
of a police raid. Government responses are also criticized in another Banksy
mural on the wall of an underpass near the Jungle camp which depicts Steve
Jobs, Apple founder and son of Syrian migrants, accompanied by the artist's
observation that Apple only existed because 'they allowed in a young man
from Homs'. The painting on a wall near Calais beach, depicts a child refugee from the Jungle gazing longingly through a telescope across the Channel

towards Britain with a vulture perched on top of the instrument. And a fourth one near the town's immigration office is a commentary on the tragic events in the Mediterranean in which Banksy re-imagines *The Raft of the Medusa* with the shipwreck survivors on the raft desperately waving to catch the attention of an ostentatious modern yacht on the horizon (UFunk, 2015; News Desk, 2016; Riotta, 2016). These depictions capture the horror of the refugee's predicament in raw brutality.

The historicized spatiality of Calais continues to shape Anglo-French border politics today. The border politics is rooted in a historicized spatiality dating back to the premodern era where Calais was a gateway for refugees in search of sanctuary in Britain yet equally a space of violent expulsion and de-racination. In more recent history, the 'century of refugees' (Marrus, 1985) was marked by unprecedented levels of forced displacement during the First World War. Equally the 'century of camps' organized and structured the Nazi and Soviet politics and society (Bauman, 1995). Sixty years after the liberation of Auschwitz, razor wire is being rolled out across Europe in a bid to control movement across space where the refugee and camps still predominate through a biopolitics of border control.

For Paul Gilroy (2004) the notion of camps operates on multiple levels as material description, a political technology that can mutate for instance between different types of camps and a metaphor for pathologies of 'race' and nation that underpin a form of thinking that is everywhere. He argues that forms of nationalism invoke a particular 'mode of belonging [that] exemplify camp thinking' with a common approach to collective solidarity with shared patterns of thinking that work through appeals to national or ethnic purity and in which politics is reconceptualized and reconstituted as 'dualistic conflict' between friends and enemies, them and us clearly articulated in European political debates about immigration that construct intrusions of blacks, Muslims and others as 'invasion' (Gilroy, 2004, p. 83). Razor wire fences, walls and moats become technologies for controlling movement across space. These very technologies which facilitated the protection of property also underpinned the expansion of capitalism (see Netz, 2004 on the historical ecology of barbed wire). In the process, these also manifest expressions of the fear of the stranger at our doors (Bauman, 2016). More specifically a primal fear invasion not by foreign armies but the racialized refugee reconstituted as the 'illegal migrant, a trespasser and disruptor of legitimate traffic of neoliberal economy (see Agier, 2016).

About this book

This chapter traced the chequered history of Calais and sought to highlight the town as a space inscribed through migrant and refugee politics over time. The second chapter reviews the history of camps in Calais both in terms of the contemporary politics of forced migration and through its historical trajectory. The jungles of Calais acquire a politicized and spatialized meaning in the contemporary landscape where the jungle co-produces a lesser humanity, both in the denial of sanctuary and in the re-coding of these entities as economic opportunists seeking to plunder the coffers in the UK. These readings as such set the premise and the measure of whether or when pity or humanity can be accorded to the inhabitants of the jungle. Chapter 3 reviews the management of migrants and refugees through the analysis of policy within the UK and EU, and how issues of sovereignty and security become dual platforms to distance themselves from the humanitarian crises at the border. The imaging and visualization of the refugee and jungle is reviewed in Chapter 4 and the increased scrutiny into their environment becomes a resonant theme in the newspaper prior to the demolition of the camps in 2016. This abundance of the media gaze produces the jungle inhabitants as objects of curiosity within a precarious setting taking extraordinary risks with their bodies and their progeny. Chapter 5 looks at the plight of children in the jungle and particularly the lack of a concerted humanitarian initiative towards unaccompanied children in the camps. Their plight is mapped against the reticent and lukewarm stance of the British government. The last chapter looks at the recurrent demolition of the camps, describing these as impotent and ineffective measures that become tools of self-gratification to assuage the public. In real terms, the current demolitions reveal the lack of a concerted policy towards the displaced in Calais. In the process, they highlight the brutality of neoliberal politics where periodic erasure seeks to affirm sovereign power and the production of bare life through the border politics of control and expulsion.

Notes

1 Juxtaposed controls are an arrangement between Belgium, France and the United Kingdom whereby immigration checks on cross-Channel routes take place before boarding the train or ferry, rather than on arrival.

2 By June 2002, the French railways and Port of Calais had spent €13.6 million upgrading security and €3 million a year on running costs (Schuster, 2003). Eurotunnel had spent £3 million on security measures including fences, razor wire, cameras and £3 million a year on security guards around the terminal site to prevent migrants and refugees boarding passing vehicles (Schuster, 2003).

3 Over the course of the nineteenth century, lace became a flourishing industry and as regular sea crossings began large numbers of Britons settled in Calais. Globalization has since 'silenced the historic looms of Calais' and blue-collar voters now 'represent the forces powering the far right' and support for Le Pen's anti-immigration National Front (Alderman, 2017).

4 An estimated 140,000 Chinese workers served on the Western Front, mostly in the British Chinese Labour Corp, and after Armistice, about 5000–7000 stayed in France, forming what was later to become the Chinese community in Paris (Fawcett, 2000).

5 Particularly during the Age of Revolutions that convulsed Europe between 1774 and 1848 Calais continued to be one of the gateways to sanctuary in Britain for nationalists and exiles from as far afield as Russia, Hungary, Italy and France. British artisans who had smuggled giant looms into Calais to get around restrictions on selling lace after the end of the Napoleonic war found themselves the targets of xenophobic attacks following the resurgence of French nationalism after the 1848 revolution. Ostracized, marginalized and financially distressed, the British lace makers at one point sought refuge on Channel ferries, and were forced to emigrate to Australia (Bensimon, 2016; Alderman, 2017).

6 The contemporary refugee crisis in Europe needs to be seen in the context of an estimated 10 million displaced internally or across borders in the First World War (Gatrell, 2008) and 60 million during and after the Second World War (Zampano, Moloney and Juan, 2015). The contemporary refugee crisis in Europe peaked in 2015 when 1 million displaced people crossed the Mediterranean in search of sanctuary in Europe, and before the phased demolition of the Jungle in 2016 it had an estimated 10,000 occupants.

7 They worked digging trenches, building transport infrastructure and after the end of the war clearing live ordnance, exhuming decomposing bodies and removing them to new war cemeteries. The work was arduous, based on 10-hour days, seven days a week and with three holidays (Kennedy, 2014). When Britain distributed 6 million commemorative medals to those who participated in the war, those handed out to the Chinese bore only their numbers, not their names, and were bronze not silver. Originally painted into a giant canvas depicting a victorious France surrounded by her allies, they were wiped out to create space for the Americans who entered the war in 1917 (Kennedy, 2014).

8 Also known as *O, the Roast Beef of Old England* was reproduced as a print from an engraving the following year and then circulated widely. Hogarth completed the painting after his return from France where he had been arrested as a spy while sketching the gate of Calais. The scene depicts a side of beef being carried from the harbour to an English tavern in the port while a group of under-nourished French soldiers and a fat friar look on hungrily.

9 The interactive mural was added to Google's digital archive, the Cultural Institute's Banksy site, moments before it was removed (McGoogan, 2016).

References

Agier, M. (2016) *Borderlands: Towards an Anthropology of the Cosmopolitan.* Edited by (tr.) David Fernback. Cambridge: Polity Press.

Alderman, L. (2017) 'Once a lace capital, now riven by French politics', *New York Times*, 29 April. Accessed 30 November 2016 at: www.nytimes.com/2017/04/29/business/france-election-globalization-lepen-macron-lace.html.

Allen, P. (2009) 'Pictured new squalid migrant camp pops up in Calais hours after the Jungle is razed'. *Daily Mail*, 24 September. Accessed 30 November 2016 at: www.dailymail.co.uk/news/article-1215568/New-squalid-migrant-camp-pops-Calais-hours-Jungle-razed.html.

Bashford, A. and McAdam, J. (2014) 'The right to asylum: Britain's 1905 Aliens Act and the evolution of refugee law'. *Law and History Review*, 32(2), pp. 309–350.

Bauman, Z. (1995) 'The century of camps', in P. Beilharz (ed.) *The Bauman Reader*. Malden, MA and Oxford: Blackwell Publishing, pp. 230–280.

Bauman, Z. (2016) *Strangers at Our Door*. Cambridge: Polity Press.

Bensimon, F. (2016) 'Calais: 1816–2016', *History Today*, 24 October. Accessed 19 November 2017 at: www.historytoday.com/fabrice-bensimon/calais-1816-2016.

Boswell, C. (2012) 'How information scarcity influences the policy agenda: Evidence from UK immigration policy'. *Governance*, 25(3), pp. 367–389.

Bracchi, P. (2009) 'Bloody siege of Calais: The violent new breed of migrants who will let nothing stop them coming to Britain'. *Mail Online*, 25 July. Accessed 30 November 2016 at: www.dailymail.co.uk/news/article-1202009/Bloody-siege-Calais-The-violent-new-breed-migrants-let-stop-coming-Britain.html#ixzz3soO3P7BV.

Bulman, M. (2017b) '"Endemic police brutality": The appalling treatment of refugees in northern France'. *The Independent*, 24 April, p. 7.

Campbell, M., Henry, R., Lyons, J. and Hookham, M. (2015) 'I tell her she's going to meet her daddy'. *The Sunday Times*, 2 August. Accessed 30 November 2016. www.thesundaytimes.co.uk/sto/news/focus/article1588471.ece.

Darian-Smith, E. (1999) *Bridging Divides: The Channel Tunnel and English Legal Identity in the New Europe*. Los Angeles, CA: University of California Press.

Davidson, J. (2000) 'The beef that made John Bull'. *The Guardian*, 25 March. Accessed 30 November 2016 at: www.theguardian.com/books/2000/mar/25/books.guardianreview7.

Fassin, D. (2012) 'Compassion and repression: The moral economy of immigration policies in France', *Cultural Anthropology*, 23(3), pp. 362–387.

Fawcett, B. (2000) 'The Chinese Labour Corp in France, 1917–1921', *Journal of the Royal Asiatic Society Hong Kong Branch*, 40, pp. 33–111.

Gatrell, P. (2008) 'Refugees and forced migrants during the First World War'. *Immigrants and Minorities*, 26(1–2), pp. 82–110.

Gatrell, P. (2014) 'Refugees'. *International Encyclopedia of the First World War*. Accessed 30 November 2016 at: https://encyclopedia.1914-1918-online.net/pdf/1914-1918-Online-refugees-2014-10-08.pdf.

Geddes, A. (2005) 'Getting the best of both worlds? Britain, the EU and migration policy'. *International Affairs*, 81(4), pp. 723–740.

Gilroy, P. (2004) *Between Camps: Nations, Cultures and the Allure of Race*. London and New York: Routledge.

Gower, M. and Smith, B. (2015) Briefing Paper: Migration pressures in Europe. 08 September. London: House of Commons Library. Accessed 14 January 2018 at: http://researchbriefings.parliament.uk/ResearchBriefing/Summary/CBP-7210#fullreport.

Griffin, N. (1976) 'Britain's Chinese Labor Corps in World War I'. *Military Affairs*, 40(3), pp. 102–108.

Gwynn, R. (1985) 'England's "first refugees"'. *History Today*, 35(5). Accessed 19 November 2017 at: www.historytoday.com/robin-gwynn/englands-first-refugees.

Hall, J. and Allen, P. (2015) 'Finally! Workers put up fences, razor wire and extra security cameras at the Eurotunnel site in France to stop people illegally reaching Britain . . . meanwhile the migrants are building HOUSES'. *Mail Online*, 5 August. Accessed 30 November 2016 at: www.dailymail.co.uk/news/article-3185994/ Finally-Workers-fences-razor-wire-extra-security-cameras-Eurotunnel-site-France-stop-people-illegally-reaching-Britain-migrants-building-HOUSES.html.

Hills, A. (2002) 'Border control services and security sector reform', *Geneva Centre for the Democratic Control of Armed Forces (DCAF) Working Paper Series*, 13, p. 319.

Hintermaier, J.M. (2000) 'The first modern refugees? Charity, entitlement and persuasion in the Huguenot immigration of the 1680s'. *Albion: A Quarterly Journal Concerned with British Studies*, 32(3), pp. 429–449.

Howarth, A. and Ibrahim, Y. (2012) 'Threat and suffering: The liminal space of "the Jungle"', in L. Roberts and H. Andrews (eds) *Liminal Landscapes: Travel, Experience and Spaces in-between*. London: Routledge, pp. 100–114.

Ibrahim, Y. and Howarth, A. (2017) 'Communicating the "migrant" Other as risk: Space, EU and expanding borders'. *Journal of Risk Research*, 17 April. Accessed 11 January 2018 at: www.tandfonline.com/doi/abs/10.1080/13669877.2017.131 3765?journalCode=rjrr20.

Janner-Klausner, L. (2015) 'When Jewish people look at Calais migrants, we see ourselves'. *The Guardian*, 13 August. Accessed 30 November 2016 at: www. theguardian.com/commentisfree/2015/aug/13/jewish-people-calais-migrants-kindertransport-children-nazis.

Kennedy, M. (2014) 'First World War's forgotten Chinese Labour Corps to get recognition at last'. *The Guardian*, 14 August. Accessed 30 November 2016 at: www.theguardian.com/world/2014/aug/14/first-world-war-forgotten-chinese-labour-corps-memorial.

Keyes, E. (2004) 'Expansion and restriction: Competing pressures on United Kingdom asylum policy'. *University of Baltimore Law*, 395. Accessed 30 November 2016 at: http://scholarworks.law.ubalt.edu/cgi/viewcontent.cgi?article=1342&context=all_ fac.

Kleingeld, P. (1998) 'Kant's cosmopolitan law: World citizenship for a global order'. *Kantian Review*, 2, pp. 72–90.

Lambert, C. L. (2011) 'Edward III's siege of Calais: A reappraisal'. *Journal of Medieval History*, 37(3), pp. 245–256.

London, L. (2000) 'Whitehall and the refugees: The 1930s and the 1990s'. *Patterns of Prejudice*, 34(3), pp. 17–26.

McGoogan, C. (2016) 'Google digitises Banksy's "Les Miserables" mural as it is taken down'. *Telegraph.co.uk*. 27 January. Accessed 11 January 2018 at: www. telegraph.co.uk/technology/2016/01/27/google-digitises-banksys-les-misrables-mural-as-it-is-taken-down/.

McGuinness, R. (2017) 'Calais Jungle RETURNS: Officials say it's LAWLESS AND DANGEROUS and deem it a "NO-GO ZONE"'. *Express Online*, 19 January. Accessed 30 November 2016 at: www.express.co.uk/news/world/756356/Calais-Jungle-returns-lawless-dangerous-no-go-zone-France-refugee-camp.

McNeil, R. (2014) 'Calais and clandestine migration into the UK: Concerns and context'. Oxford: Oxford Migration Observatory, 24 October. Accessed 30 November 2016 at: www.migrationobservatory.ox.ac.uk/commentary/calais-and-clandestine-migration-uk-concerns-and-context.

Marrus, M.R. (1985) *The Unwanted: European Refugees in the Twentieth Century*. Oxford: Oxford University Press.

Minca, C. (2015) 'Geographies of the camp'. *Political Geography*, 49, pp. 74–83.

Netz, R. (2004) *Barbed Wire: An Ecology of Modernity*. Durham, NC: Wesleyan University Press.

News Desk (2016) 'Banksy returns for refugees'. *World Bulletin*, 12 December. Accessed 19 November 2017 at: www.worldbulletin.net/world/167307/banksy-returns-for-refugees.

Nord-Pas-de-Calais (no date) 'Chinese labourers in Northern France during the Great War'. Accessed 30 November 2016 at: www.remembrancetrails-northernfrance.com/history/nations-in-war/chinese-labourers-in-northern-france-during-the-great-war.html.

Panikos, P. (2011) 'Imperial collapse and the creation of refugees in twentieth-century Europe', in P. Panayi and P. Virdee (eds) *Refugees and the End of Empire: Imperial Collapse and Forced Migration*. Basingstoke: Palgrave Macmillan, pp. 3–27.

Papademetriou, D. (2015) 'Top 10 of 2015 – Issue # 1: Migration crisis tests European consensus and governance'. *Migration Policy Institute*, 18 December. Accessed 30 November 2016 at: www.migrationpolicy.org/article/top-10-2015-issue-1-migration-crisis-tests-european-consensus-and-governance.

Powley, T. and Stacey, K. (2015) 'Calais migrants: hauliers fear Channel tunnel night closure plans'. *Financial Times*, 7 August. Accessed 30 November 2016 at: www.ft.com/cms/s/0/3704b50c-3cf8-11e5-bbd1-b37bc06f590c.html.

Readman, P. (2014a) '"The cliffs are not cliffs": The cliffs of Dover and national identities in Britain'. *History*, 99(335), pp. 241–269.

Riotta, C. (2016) 'Banksy "Les Misérables" art about Calais refugee camp appears on French Embassy in London'. *News.Mic*, 24 January. Accessed 30 November 2016 at: https://mic.com/articles/133354/banksy-les-mis-rables-art-about-calais-refugee-camp-appears-on-french-embassy-in-london#.kaRazPsGu.

Roberts, M.R. (2010) '"Footprints in the concrete": A study of the Chemin des Juifs (Jews' Road), Jewish slave labour camps, and related sites, in the Nord-Pas-de-Calais, France'. *The Historic Environment: Policy and Practice*, 1(1), pp. 70–102.

Robinson, J. (2016) 'Ripped to pieces: Dramatic aerial images reveal how the Calais Jungle is being torn down just weeks after the squalid camp was packed with thousands of tents and huts'. *MailOnline*. 28 October. Accessed 11 January 2018 at: www.dailymail.co.uk/news/article-3882566/Ripped-pieces-Dramatic-aerial-images-reveal-Calais-Jungle-torn-just-weeks-squalid-camp-packed-thousands-tents-huts.html.

Rose, S. (2008) *Calais: An English Town in France, 1347–1558*. Woodbridge: Boydell Press.

Rygiel, K. (2011) 'Bordering solidarities: Migrant activism and the politics of movement and camps at Calais'. *Citizenship Studies*, 15(1), pp. 1–19.

Schuster, L. (2003) 'Asylum seekers: Sangatte and the Tunnel'. *Parliamentary Affairs*, 56(3), pp. 506–522+ii+v.

Shakespeare, W. (1993) *Richard II* in J. Hylton (ed). *Complete Works of Shakespeare*. The Tech: MIT. Accessed 13 December 2017. at: http://shakespeare.mit.edu/richardii/richardii.2.1.html.

Shaw, C. (2015) *Britannia's Embrace: Modern Humanitarianism and the Imperial Origins of Refugee Relief*. Oxford: Oxford University Press.

Sheldrick, G. (2017) '"Another summer of HELL": Violent traffickers smuggling migrants into Britain EXPOSED'. *Express Online*, 25 March. Accessed 30 November 2016 at: www.express.co.uk/news/uk/783668/Violent-traffickers-smuggling-migrants-Britain.

Sparks, I. (2015) 'Calais is the most right wing town in France: Marine Le Pen's National Front score massive 49 per cent of votes in the home of the Jungle'. *Daily Mail*, 9 December. Accessed 30 November 2016 at: www.dailymail.co.uk/news/article-3353002/Calais-Right-wing-town-France-Marine-Le-Pen-s-National-score-massive-49-cent-votes-home-Jungle.html#ixzz3tu1j8LcJ.

Stone, D. (2017) *Concentration Camps: A Short History*. Oxford: Oxford University Press.

Stothard, M. (2015) 'As Calais shanty town for UK-bound migrants grows, winter looms'. *Financial Times*, 30 October. Accessed 30 November 2016 at: www.ft.com/cms/s/0/82253e90-7e60-11e5-a1fe-567b37f80b64.html.

The Guardian Staff (2002) 'Sangatte refugee camp'. *Guardian*, 23 May. Accessed 30 November 2016 at: www.theguardian.com/uk/2002/may/23/immigration.immigrationandpublicservices1.

The Times (2015) 'Trouble across the water (Leading Article)', 30 July. Accessed 30 November 2016 at: www.thetimes.co.uk/tto/opinion/leaders/article4513137.ece.

Thornhill, T. (2014) 'Calais under siege: Migrants march through streets demanding human rights protection amid warnings French port is being overwhelmed'. *Mail Online*, 8 October. Accessed 30 November 2016 at: www.dailymail.co.uk/news/article-2744837/Alarming-footage-emerges-migrants-vaulting-16-foot-fence-ferries-Calais-amid-warnings-shutting-port-just-problem-elsewhere.html.

UFunk (2015) 'Banksy invites himself in Calais with four new street art creations for the migrants'. *Blog*, 12 December. Accessed 30 November 2016 at: www.ufunk.net/en/artistes/banksy-calais-migrants/.

Vanfleteren, S. (2014) 'The ghostly remains of Nazi Germany's Atlantic Wall'. *Time*, 15 August. Accessed 30 November 2016 at: http://time.com/3387172/the-ghostly-remains-of-nazi-germanys-atlantic-wall/.

Wallace, D. (2008) *Premodern Places: Calais to Surinam, Chaucer to Aphra Behn*. Malden, MA and Oxford: Blackwell Publishing.

Wigg, G. (1949) *Hansard* HC Debate. Vol. 467 col. 2846.

Zampano, G., Moloney, L. and Juan, J. (2015) 'Migrant crisis: A history of displacement'. *Wall Street Journal*, 22 September. Accessed 30 November 2016 at: http://graphics.wsj.com/migrant-crisis-a-history-of-displacement/.

Zaretsky, R. (2015) 'A moat defensive'. *Foreign Policy (Blog)*. Accessed 30 November 2016 at: http://foreignpolicy.com/2015/07/31/a-moat-defensive-english-channel-separating-migrants-calais/.

2 The camp and the 'Jungle'

Introduction

The camp as a site of transience and madness but more importantly the disregard for life and denigration is a starting point of enquiry in this chapter. As a container of transient human life yet not fully accorded any protection beyond its borders, the camp is constituted as a complex and polysemic site where 'bare life' is produced and where states of exception can be applied (Agamben, 1998). Since the 1980s, assumptions and discourses about the rights of refugees to protection have been eroded as governments have struggled to deal with increases in unregulated mass migration, people trafficking and international terrorism (Geddes, 2005; Bosworth, 2012). States, rather than offering sanctuary, have reframed migration as involving 'risky outsiders and threatened insiders' and refugees as migrants (Millner, 2011). A security–judicial apparatus has grown up around tighter border controls aimed at keeping migrants out and criminalizing 'certain forms of movement . . . [so] effectively rendering large proportions of the world's population as illegal' (Aas, 2011, p. 26). 'New spaces' have emerged both to detain migrants during the asylum process and as informal camps of makeshift shelters erected by migrants on wasteland or in disused industrial buildings in towns and cities (Isin, Engin and Rygiel, 2007, p. 171). The security–judicial border controls render these as spaces of exception where the usual rights and protections afforded refugees or citizens are denied to those suspected of being illegal migrants. These include the right not to be detained as well as the right to shelter and to welfare benefits (Isin, Engin and Rygiel, 2007; Aas, 2011).

Spaces can be socially, materially and discursively constructed (Harvey, 1973). Shields conceptualizes this spatialization as a 'social imaginary' where spatial divisions and distinctions provide the means to ground hegemonic ideologies and social practices (1999). In these 'social imaginaries' issues of belonging, boundaries and othering can reflect discursive and material practices of 'us' and 'them', exclusion and inclusion. More recent literature has developed this further, arguing that landscapes and dominant features in these 'become spatially bounded scenes that visually communicate what belongs and what does not' (Trudeau, 2006, p. 421). They thus become critical to the construction of a 'territorialized politics of belonging' in which the discourses and practices that maintain boundaries 'correspond to the imagined geographies of a polity and to the spaces that normatively embody the polity' (Trudeau, 2006, p. 421).

The politics of territoriality has taken a particular form with 'Fortress Europe', a term that conveys the sense of a space under siege from waves of irregular migration, the response to which has been the tightening of the security–judicial apparatus on the EU's external borders (Bosworth and Guild, 2008, p. 213). Recent legal changes require migrants to apply for asylum at the point of entry but most wait until they reach their preferred destination – often Germany and the UK – so as many as 90 per cent may be illegal under the new laws (Oxfam cf. Millner, 2011, p. 236). The EU has also relaxed internal borders under the Schengen Agreement which allows free, undocumented travel between signatory countries. Britain opted out of the Agreement and retained border controls, the consequence of which has been to render the French coastline the 'extreme periphery' of the Schengen area and a site of relatively large congregations of migrants seeking to cross the sea border (Ibrahim and Howarth, 2015; Thomas, 2013). Calais has seen a particular concentration of migrants because of its multi-modal transport links (i.e. ferry, train and lorry) that offer more opportunities for stowaways. As such, this renders Calais as a key site of cross-border tension as well as cooperation between the two countries.

French politicians blame the 'problem' of large numbers of migrants in Calais on what they see as a clash between the attraction of Britain's over-generous benefit system and 'inhumane' border controls that block movement across the Channel, thus creating a bottleneck on their side of the border (Howarth and Ibrahim, 2012). Conversely, British politicians blame France for loose border controls, summed up in expressions such as '"we don't have a barrier, we have a sieve"' (Damien Green cf. Bosworth and Guild, 2008, p. 704). Both governments have responded by seeking to deter migrants with more surveillance and tighter border controls in Calais (Mulvey, 2010) and a raft of new laws but rather than solve the problem it has created the sense of a 'system . . . in perpetual crisis'; both governments 'lost control of the debate' and British media hostility towards migrants hardened (Mulvey, 2010, p. 456).

It is within this context of crisis that the jungle metaphor was applied by newspapers to the migrant camps on the French coastline. Rygiel has argued that Europe's migrant camps are 'sites of contestation' so their 'very meaning' needs to be explored (2011, p. 1). At one level, the meaning of camps studied in this article is functional: they are located near major transit areas that present migrants with opportunities to leap onto passing vehicles headed across the Channel and they meet the basic need for shelter. However, the camps are also visible symbols of the presence of migrants, the scale of migration and hence failed migration policies (Ibrahim, 2011; Boswell, 2012; Howarth and Ibrahim, 2012). These two elements converged in the row over Sangatte Red Cross Centre which closed in 2002 after a riot and pressure from the British government which argued that such shelters acted as a magnet for more migrants (Boswell, 2012b). This marked the beginning of a sustained policy in which charities were allowed to provide food, hot showers and basic medical care but not migrant shelters, which were closed, banned or demolished (Bulman, 2017a). This fragmented policy forced them to erect their own makeshift shelters. The sprouting of these makeshift camps between 2007 and 2011 saw the emergence of the spatial metaphor of the jungle.

The closure of Sangatte brought British newspaper attention on Calais as a major conduit for cross-channel illegal migration (Boswell, 2012). The row over the shelter became a 'focusing event' that grounded and concretized the more elusive problem of illegal migration for journalists (Boswell, 2012). It also gave impetus to a decade-long campaign by British newspapers particularly in the two mid-market titles, the *Daily Mail* and *Express*, on illegal migration (see Ibrahim, 2011; Howarth and Ibrahim, 2012). Editors have argued that their campaigns were in the interest of their readers because the scale of migration posed major demographic changes and because of the failure of government to solve the problem. However human rights organizations and analysts counter that coverage has drawn on 'de-humanizing' labels for migrants and created a 'misleading picture' of immigration 'fuelling political prejudice and extremism' in Britain (Commission for Racial Equality, 2007, p. 98).

The Western social imaginary of the jungle

The jungles of Calais are a referential in the migration crisis not because they have any distinctive material realities, features or possibilities for political agency; much of what was and is there can be found in other formal and informal refugee camps (see Ramadan, 2013; Katz, 2015; Minca, 2015a; Agier, 2016). The distinctiveness of the Calais camps lies mainly in the 'colonial leitmotif' of the jungle (Zaretsky, 2015) imbued as it is with a distinctively Western social imaginary that renders explicit the ontologies of camp thinking identified by Gilroy and becomes politically and racially charged when affixed to camps inhabited by refugees from former colonies.

The meaning ascribed to the jungle is not that of reality television shows or exotic safaris where tourists venture into the bush accompanied by armed guides for protection from poachers or wild animals, but derived from a longer social imaginary rooted in a colonial construct about the spaces inhabited by the 'other'. The word 'jungle' originated form the Sanskrit *jangala* which in the pre-colonized Indian sub-continent had both a normative and descriptive meaning of 'culturally desirable' savanna viewed by the ancient state as indicating the presence of civilization (Dove, 1992, p. 231). However, with time the word evolved to mean the 'culturally undesirable . . . forest waste' and after colonization morphed into the Anglo-Indian word jungle where flora and fauna were reconstructed as 'feral', as were the people who lived in or near the jungle, and for the colonial administration it signified the absence of civilization (Dove, 1992, p. 231, 239). Similar negative associations are clearly discernible in accounts of the stench of human waste and rotting food in the jungles of Calais (*Daily Mail* Reporter, 2009; Hughes and Spooner, 2016), the 'feral' children and brutality of the 'jungle rape camp' (Peake 2008; Sinmaz 2016) and the 'law of the jungle' which demolition was intended to bring to an end (Bracchi, 2009; *The Times*, 2016).

The persistence of the colonialist trope of the jungle in the social imaginary of the spaces inhabited by the other has been sustained in part by an ongoing fascination for the Western mind with the 'jungle' (Rose, 2016). The fascination has been kept alive in multiple forms of popular culture from Rudyard Kipling's *Jungle Book* (1893) to the videogame *Jumanji: The Jungle* (2017). Films centred on characters such as Tarzan or Jake Sully in *Avatar* perpetuate in the social imaginary the racial hierarchy of the dominant white male in unfathomable and dangerous jungles, able to distinguish themselves from the 'natives' by a natural authority and physical prowess (Rose, 2016). Post-colonial author Chinua Achebe argues the continuing fascination in the west with the dominant conception of Africa constructed in Joseph Conrad's *Heart of Darkness* arises in part out of a need to set the continent up as a 'foil to Europe . . . the antithesis of Europe and therefore of civilization, a place where man's vaunted intelligence and refinement are finally mocked by triumphant bestiality' (Achebe, 1977, p. 3). For Achebe, Africa and Conrad's jungle as setting or backdrop 'eliminates the African as a human factor', dehumanizing and depersonalizing a 'portion of the human race' (Achebe, 1977, p. 9).

The other dimension to the colonial leitmotif is a dialectic in which (white) humans shape the jungle but the jungle also shapes them. The protagonist hero, Tarzan or Sully, respectively resist the primordial temptations of the jungle that would lead to a reversion to a primitive self while the fallen succumbs so that the darkness within melds with the darkness without. The revelation of the 'horror' in *Heart of Darkness* is when the individual becomes debased and what is revealed is not that of a common humanity, but a behavioural reversion to the pre-modern savage indistinguishable from the 'native' in all but pigmentation. The jungle in much of this popular culture is a pre-modern space of degradation, debasement and barbarism, the antithesis of Enlightened Europe. The impulse of colonialism was to tame the wild, bring order to a primordial chaos and push back at the natural tendency of the jungle to encroach on the civilized. A reversion to the state of jungle entailed a loss of control of space, landscape and inhabitants to the dangerous, the untamed and primitive. Mowgli's revenge in *The Jungle Book* was to 'let in' the jungle to a place that 'had been under the plough not six months before' (Kipling, 1999, p. 207, 212, cf. Dove, 1992, p. 240) and the punishment for a moral violation was the unchecked growth of vegetation.

Embedded in the colonial construct is a primal fear of the Other and spaces out of which they come. As the voice-over in one of the Tarzan films says, 'The jungle consumes everything . . . it preys on the old, the sick and wounded. It preys on the weak – but never the strong' (Rose, 2016). The primal fear is most acute when the 'white man in the jungle' is inverted and the mobile black body brings the 'Dark Continent' into Europe. In the film and video game *Jumanji* the jungle is unleashed in the middle of white suburbia and in documentaries such as *Killer Virus* and *Plague Doctors*, where lethal viruses transmitted from the tropics to the West are said to threaten to replace 'civilization with the savagery of the jungle' (Bass, 1998, p. 432). Perhaps the most explicit expression of this primal fear is *Camp of Saints*, a dystopian, anti-immigration novel by French author Jean Raspail published in 1975 that predicts the end of the West after an 'invasion' of Europe by Indian migrants crossing the Mediterranean in flimsy, overcrowded boats seeking to escape poverty. Belated action by French government is not enough and Western civilization is overrun. The book has been labelled 'stunningly racist' in that characterization is constructed wholly through race and it 'reframes everything as a fight to the death between races' (Blumenthal and Rieger, 2017). The book has long been a 'cult classic among white supremacists' in America and Europe and was evoked after Jungle 1 was demolished in 2009 in a warning by a newspaper columnist that the 'tide of despair has only just begun' (Johnston, 2009).[1]

These political and social contexts shaped the conditions for a particular social imaginary of the jungle in British newspaper discourses between 2007 and 2010. The spatial–political dimension created a sense of space under threat, in crisis and the corresponding response of governments as being inadequate. At the same time there was a politicization of and increased media attention on migrant shelters and the spaces where these sprung up.

The metaphor of the jungle created a distinct 'othering' of migrants as lesser humans. Edward Said (1978) in his study of Orientalism observes how outsiders can impose associations and connotations on the identities of people by manipulating or coalescing traits and attributes. The metaphor of the jungle created a spatial category in which to isolate the migrant and demark him or her as different from the civilized population.

Camp as transient life

For Agamben, the twentieth century saw the figure of the refugee emerge as a mass phenomenon. In the case of Calais, the metaphor of the jungle collapses distinctions between animal and man, reducing its inhabitants through the primitive and primordial lens where the body and its senses can be continuously depleted of basic amenities and dignity or any recognition of their lives and those of their progeny as sacred (Ibrahim and Howarth, 2014). The jungle of Calais constitutes a border politics of insatiable violence where sovereign authority can be exercised without impunity. However, the jungle of Calais also functions beyond Agamben's immaculate conception of 'bare life'. The Jungle is untamed, vigorous and the more you cut it down, the more it grows, challenging its oppressors.

Hence, the story of the jungle in Calais is about the constant making and unmaking of the camp. It is like a bad dream on a loop for the authorities where every demolition is about the sprouting of new camps and tactics to avoid and evade police brutality and harassment. As such, the jungle is both about its fragility and resilience harbouring the precarious, yet also relentlessly challenging the authorities with its reincarnation and rebirth. These recurring camps are an aesthetic blight for the urban psyche where they perform as the 'broken windows' on white suburbia. The metaphor of the jungle also speaks of transcendence where it has the power to turn white suburbia into the untamed and uncouth. The terminology of the jungle as such conveys both the extreme threat it poses through its difference and equally its ability to denigrate space through the presence of the displaced body. Its aesthetic dissonance then calls out for its sustained annihilation as it is a marker of both bodily and spatial violation in Calais. The demolition of the camp was partly legitimized to 'rid' Calais of refugees and it was partly justified in terms of putting an end to the 'law of the jungle' (see Bracchi, 2009).

As discussed in the earlier chapter, Calais is a space that is constantly a transit point for countless cohorts of people during different periods in history. Its identity is about this unsettled nature of the passage of people travelling through and owning it periodically in various times in history. Calais at various times and in different incarnations has been inhabited by refugees and migrants with its most recent precursors during the Balkans conflict of the 1990s (Schwenken, 2014). The significance of the contemporary 'migrant crisis' facing Europe is often explained in popular commentary in numerical terms as the biggest since the Second World War (see for example, Reid, 2016). The previous chapter though mapped trends that are deeper and longer. The expulsion of the Ashkenazi Jews of Eastern Europe in the 1880s marked the beginnings of mass displacement and with two world wars the number of displaced people increased 'astronomically' to the point that the twentieth century came to be referenced by historians as the 'century of refugees' (Marrus, 1985). It prompted Zygmunt Bauman (1995) to ponder whether it could also be termed as the 'century of camps' where beyond their proliferation, the biopolitical technologies of camps became the organizing principles that structured entire societies and controlled the lives of millions of people. Claudio Minca (2015b) reiterates a similar argument by drawing attention to the cartographic parallels between a network of concentration camps and gulags that criss-crossed Nazi Germany and the Soviet Union and the network of detention centres for 'failed' asylum seekers that now dot the EU.

The Cambridge Dictionary denotes the meaning of the camp as 'a place where people stay in tents or other temporary structures' and an area where people are 'kept' temporarily for a reason. The refugee camp, detention centre and concentration camp can be fundamentally different, but delineating the distinctions is problematic as physical features differ even between concentration camps (cf. Netz, 2004; Stone, 2017). While the jungle as a refugee camp is a different spatial formation to the concentration camp, their histories overlap in several ways. The two defining features of the twentieth century, the figure of the refugee and the camp, came together with modern biopolitical technologies during the Anglo-Boer War of 1899–1902 in South Africa. The British, faced with the prospect of losing the war against more mobile Boer commandos, adopted new strategies to control space (Netz, 2004). Not only did they roll out barbed wire across thousands of miles of bushveld to slow the movement of the commandos, they also burnt down Boer farm land and buildings to deprive the enemy of a source of food. The women and children occupying the farms were rounded up along with the cattle and herded into what the British called 'refugee camps' with the intent of saving them from starvation. These squalid, disease-ridden camps became a national scandal in Britain but till today such conditions remain a distinct feature of refugee camps. Initially, the civilians were contained but not incarcerated. As unenclosed formations, its inhabitants were free to come and go but the scarcity of food beyond the camp meant few ventured forth. It was only after Boer commandos had raided the camp for cattle that barbed wire, an invention of the colonization and subjugation of the American west, was erected around the camps, effectively imprisoning the occupants (Stone, 2017). These became 'concentration camps' holding incarcerated refugees behind barbed wire or a fortified enclosure. The key difference between concentration camps and refugee camps is in the degree of overt compulsion. The incarcerated are 'kept' and their movement restricted to within the camp while in most refugee camps or reception centres the inhabitants are free to come and go but their mobility beyond the camp may be constrained by border controls, razor wire and walls.

The Nazis imported the biopolitical technology of the concentration camp from the colonies into Europe; nevertheless, the stigma of these predate the Nazis (see Stone, 2017). During the First World War, some governments grappling with mass displacement of people were concerned that the public would draw parallels with the infamous concentration camps of the Anglo-Boer War and took care to label these as refugee camps even where there was de facto incarceration (see Thorpe, 2011). The response of the sovereign power to a massive influx of refugees is not without constraints, but these were additionally mediated by the perceptions of the public sphere. The Anglo-Boer War also demonstrated that the spatial formation of the camp is not static but one that evolves over time in response to a wider context and actions, internal and external to it. This then presents difficulties in attributing defining features to the camps. Barbed wire and watch-towers may be definitive features of Auschwitz, but these were neither needed nor present in some of the gulags of Siberia where inhospitable conditions and the harsh weather coalesced, seamlessly presenting a concerted barrier against escapes (see Stone, 2017).

Razor wire encircled the detention centre in Woomera and refugee camps in Macedonia in late 1990s (Pugliese, 2002; Stoddart, 2006; Figure 2.1) but were not formally used to enclose the jungles of Calais although volunteers working for Médicins Sans Frontières (MSF) noted the increasing containment around these camps. According to volunteers reflecting on these camps in 2016, 'we would find new fences, new walls and new areas where trees were cut down to enable police surveillance of residents' and they opined that 'surrounded by barriers on all sides' and built on a former industrial waste site, the jungle was 'no place to live' (Drogoul and Hanryon, 2016). In the case of the jungle, the biopolitical technology of the razor wire served primarily to protect passing hauliers and Eurotunnel 'property' from incursions by migrants and refugees seeking to cross the Channel. The effect, though, was the fortification of Calais with barbed/razor wire, walls and moats as mechanisms to contain and dispel the displaced body.

The one thing all camps have in common is temporality; they are intended to be interim, provisional and makeshift. For some refugee camps, such as the Palestinian camps in Lebanon, temporality is marked through a

Figure 2.1 Sunshine on razor wire
Source: McPherson, 2012. Creative Commons Attribution 2.0 Generic licence.

'permanent impermanence' where a person may spend their entire life from birth to death as a refugee (Ramadan, 2013). In contrast, the jungle camps of Calais have a life span of no more than two to three years and as soon as they take the form of a quasi-permanent settlement they are demolished. Agamben's 'state of exception' is often used in theorizations of camps but others have pointed out that there are limitations in applying the philosopher's framework to camps that emerge 'spontaneously' and where forms of political action, self-organization and resistance can emerge when sovereign power is temporarily vacated (Ramadan, 2013; Minca, 2015a; Katz, 2015). Nevertheless, such proto-political and civic agency emerges in a hiatus and will confront the reassertion of sovereign power and the re-colonization of the space. Paul Gilroy (2004, p. 83) in his call for a continued reflection on camps and 'camp thinking' with their roots firmly lodged in colonialism, fascism and capitalism, argues that such mentalities are 'constituted by appeals to race, nation and ethic differences' and 'fantasies' of cultural identity (Gilroy, 2004, p. 83). These techniques of possession and dispossession serve to draw on the primordial while fracturing the possibilities for solidarity among humanity.

Locating the Jungle as a camp

Agamben (1998, p. 89), in referring to the concentration camps of the late nineteenth and early twentieth centuries, speaks of their inhabitants as being stripped of every political status and reduced completely to naked life. The camp is the most absolute biopolitical space that has ever been realized – a space in which power confronts nothing other than pure biological life without any mediation. Whereas the space of the exception was once localized in spaces such as the camps, Agamben implies that in more recent times it has become more widespread or generalized in contemporary political life: 'The camp, which is now firmly settled inside [the nation-state], is the new biopolitical nomos of the planet' (1989, p. 93). As such the camp rather than the city has become the biopolitical paradigm of the West, as the state of exception tends to become the rule (1996).

Agamben's spatial theory of power, sovereignty and displacement also invokes scrutiny of traditional political geographical theories about inclusion and exclusion, belonging and insularity, as well as established imaginations about thematically specific political places such as humanitarian camps (Elden, 2006). The territorial states of the 'West', generally regarded in political theory as havens of human rights and enlightened democracy Slater, 2004), have increasingly implemented harsher immigration and asylum policies. Agamben's theorization also constitutes a distinct spatial understanding of power (Minca, 2005) that calls for an examination and rereading of the political and the spatial, and more specifically the spatial logic of the camp (Diken and Laustsen, 2005).

Contextualizing the making, unmaking, and remaking of the jungle camps of Calais through Agamben's 'state of exception' allows a consideration of the implications of the state of emergency declared by the French state after the Paris attacks in 2015. The state of emergency assumed an 'escalatory dynamic' in which not only was it extended four times but the powers granted in exceptional circumstances to fight terrorism were expanded to include 'maintaining public order' including among refugees (Zaretsky, 2016). This unleashed a politics of depletion in which the inhabitants of the Jungle were denied access to legal advice during its demolition in 2016 (Bulman, 2016) and subsequently to the essentials needed to sustain life, including food (Gutteridge, 2017). As police harassment and brutality against refugees and migrants escalated, Amnesty International warned that French human rights had reached a 'tipping point' under the state of emergency (Bulman, 2017b; Dearden, 2017). The politics of depletion and brutality served to communicate that the 'unwanted' were unwelcome (see Chapter 1).

Agamben (1998, 2005) argues that a state of exception initially arises during a state of emergency where the sovereign power suspends laws, norms and conventions from a category of people, but this state of exception becomes normalized. Those stripped of political rights are denied protection from the arbitrary power of state afforded to citizens and with the divorcing of their political life from biological life, these entities are reduced to bare life. Agamben's state of exception has offered some useful insights in the exploration of spaces of incarceration and containment particularly concentration camps, gulags and detention centres (Kolosov, 2015). While it has also been applied to refugee camps, there is a growing scepticism as to whether the emerging empirical knowledge supports the application of Agamben's theory to the organic yet temporary camps that sprout spontaneously and have a different spatiality to enclosed, more institutionalized camps (Minca, 2015a).

Auschwitz as the dominant symbol of concentration–extermination camp has to some measure eclipsed the diversity of camps in the Nazi or Gulag system and their evolutionary nature (see Stone, 2017). There have been attempts to apply Agamben's space of exception not only to concentration camps and detention centres at Guantanamo Bay (cf. Gregory, 2006) but also to more spontaneous encampments of refugees that grow up organically. Agamben himself has applied the theory to refugees but such attempts have been increasingly critiqued in studies that argue while elements of Agamben's theory may be relevant it is problematic to do so to informal camps of refugees that emerge organically, are self-organizing and where sovereign power vacates the space within the camp rather than intensifies within (Minca, 2015a; Kolosov, 2015).

While the Calais camps can be located within a broader politics of a state of exception, they are not reducible to that conceptualization alone. The Jungles were not initially spaces that denoted the intensification of sovereign power. In effect, there was a withdrawal of the state from the jungle in an overarching politics of abandonment.[2] The lack of police presence in maintaining law and order within the camp facilitated its descent into the brutality of nightly violence of ethnic gang fights over resources and territory and the gang rape of women and children (Chrisafis, 2015). With increasing numbers converging into these camps, there was overcrowding and in tandem an abdication of state responsibility for basic amenities such as sanitation, lighting and refuse collection. This contributed significantly to the environmental descent of the space into rat-infested squalor, the stench of human waste and rotting food, endemic infestations of lice and contaminated water points (Isakjee, Davies and Dhesi, 2015). While brutality and degradation were defining features of all the jungle camps, the potential for a self-organizing, nascent civic and community life was most clearly manifest in Jungle 2 (2015–2016). Supported by a range of actors that entered the void left by the vacated state, religious communities within the camp assembled makeshift places of worship, cafés emerged as gathering places where volunteers could meet with refugees particularly children and shops and food hawkers sup-plemented hot meals provided by charities (Wainwright, 2016; Figure 2.2). Familiar faces of volunteers, aid workers and elders also kept a monitor-ing and watchful gaze over the most vulnerable inhabitants of the camp, the unaccompanied children. The importance of these spaces was recognized by the court which held that they were essential for community life and could not be demolished during the dismantling of the southern part of the camp in early 2016 (Agerholm, 2016).

In addition to a nascent civic life, an inchoate form of political life between the humanitarian–legal activism and citizenship emerged from the inhabitants of the jungle. As Adam Ramadan, writing on the Palestinian camps in Lebanon, has noted, spaces of 'sovereign abandonment' get filled with 'an alternative order (sometimes disorder) that can have the capacity to produce its own political life' (Ramadan, 2013, p. 72). In the jungle, this was manifest in peaceful protests in 2015, demanding their human rights be recognized and an end to police harassment, and violent protests in 2016 against the closure of the camp. The refugee camp has the potential to 'become a space in-between exception and dissent' in which refugees can speak and act in ways that, while qualified and limited, resist their

Figure 2.2 The entrance to St Michael's Church in the Calais Jungle
Source: Liam Stoopdice. 20 February 2016. © BY-SA 4.0 International license.

dehumanization (Puggioni, 2006, p. 68, 72). These are not the 'silenced and disempowered *homines sacri*' of Agamben, but nor are they the fully empowered citizen. What agency they do have is also manifest in the constant making, unmaking and remaking of the camps, a refusal to accept that they are not wanted in that space.

The reassertion of sovereign power and control over the camps was a violent one, entailing the forcible break-up of the jungle communities with the inhabitants dispersed around the country, the camp demolished and erased. Erasure was not only of a 'tented settlement', it was also of the community structures that supported men, women and children and the dislocation of the political agency of collective action. For some refugees, it was not only their shelters that were destroyed but also their possessions. Reduced to destitution and undocumented by the actions of the state, dispersed and isolated, no longer under the watchful gaze of aid workers and volunteers, their lives became harder and the children more vulnerable to sex trafficking and exploitation. The space of exception was not the jungle but the spaces beyond it, in the so-called 'civilized order' where the presence of refugees and migrants was overtly 'unwanted' (McGuiness, 2016) and police brutality was 'endemic' (Bulman, 2017b). Salient parallels can be drawn with Adam Ramadan's account of the Palestinian camps in Lebanon in which he argues that when the makeshift settlements and their communities are dismantled the inhabitants are 'reduced to something more like bare life' (Ramadan 2013, p. 72).

Space, movement and 'camp thinking'

The jungles of Calais have never been containment or incarceration camps in the literal sense. Unlike the refugee camps during the Balkans conflict or Woomera detention centre in Australia, they are not formally encircled with barbed/razor wire but became incrementally so during 2016. The inhabitants of the jungle were free to come and go as they chose. However, it is the movement of refugees and migrants across the space beyond the camps that has been increasingly curtailed. A £12 million-plus investment by the British government in 'security fencing' topped with barbed/razor wire followed by the erection of a wall along the main access routes to the port have effectively turned Calais into a 'fortress' (Taylor *et al.*, 2015). In addition, enclavic waiting spaces surrounded by barbed wire were created to 'protect' truckers and hauliers from refugees or migrants who sought to stow aboard and in early 2016 the company flooded the land around the entrance to Eurotunnel effectively creating a moat to deter incursions onto their land and onto the tracks (Ibrahim and Howarth, 2017). These biopolitical technologies of control, a combination of modern invention and ancient defences, are intended to impede the body of the refugee from moving across space, to protect property from incursions and ensure the unimpeded movement of 'legitimate' traffic.

Reviel Netz (2004) in his seminal book on the ecology of barbed wire sees that and the camp as part of the same ecology of modernity. Modern capitalism was rooted in the discovery that the private ownership of land encouraged investment but to realize the higher profits this could bring, property needed to be protected from trespassers. The urge to 'bring space under control' through enclosure first in Britain then America were key to the development of capitalism (Netz, 2004, p. 51). It was the invention of barbed wire that supported the aim of total control of space and movement across it. The barbed wire served as a biopolitical tool of control by puncturing the skin, activating the pain receptors underneath, and triggering an instant recoil eventually educating animal and human to avoid the fence. Furthermore, the barbed wire in facing both ways functioned to hold the animal inside the enclosure and to keep trespasses off the property.

As a biopolitical technology, barbed wire was highly versatile. Cheap and light, barbed wire was rolled out rapidly across vast spaces of the Great Plains facilitating the colonization of the American West and the subjugation of the Native American. However, it was during the Anglo-Boer war that barbed wire transitioned from agricultural use to warfare and where it was used against both armed combatants and unarmed humans, turning both into recipients of violence who are 'reduced to flesh and in a sense become a mere biological receptacle for pain and disease' (Netz, 2004, p. 130). The British used barbed wire to bring the movement of Boer guerrillas across vast spaces under control and to encircle what the British originally called a 'refugee camp' housing women and children unable to feed themselves after the British army had burnt down farm buildings and land, then later a 'concentration camp'.

Nazism brought the biopolitical technologies experimented on in the colonies to Europe. As with other colonial powers including Britain they entailed a construction of the Other within a biological hierarchy and in which the Other was dehumanized. Paul Gilroy (2004) argues that an understanding of the 'Nazi archipelago of concentration camps' and their victims needs to be within the histories of colonialism, capitalism and 'camp thinking'. That is, 'the camp mentalities' are rooted in 'fundamentally racist ontologies' expressed in appeals to racial, ethnic and national differences but at times racial categories have been replaced by cultural ones and resistance to difference is rooted in the 'fantasies of absolute cultural identities' (Gilroy, 2004, p. 78). For Gilroy, the nation state is all too often conceived as a sort of 'camp', 'an orderly field of people and culture to be cultivated, controlled, protected and preserved to avoid contamination and corruption'

(p. 78). A camp is also an 'experimental laboratory where life has been and continues to be inscribed into order, into real and imagined spaces.

Notes

1 There has been a resurgence of interest in the book particularly in America after the election of Donald Trump. His chief strategist Stephen Bannon uses the 'camp of saints' as a metaphor for the contemporary refugee crisis which he views as an 'invasion' by migrants (Blumenthal and Rieger, 2017).

2 The response of the authorities to the Jungle contrasted with the last months of Sangatte when armed police patrolled inside the shelter on an iron platform overlooking refugees in a bid to manage ethnic tensions. Such a spectre (and the labelling of Sangatte a camp) evoked memories of the transit camps used to hold French Jews before sending them to Auschwitz and opened the Red Cross to accusations of 'collaboration with repressive policies' (Fassin, 2012, p. 363). The justification provided by Interior Minister Nicolas Sarkozy behind closing the camp in 2002 synthesized objections to it. He argued it had become a 'magnet for illegal immigration' so drew on a classic right-wing argument for tighter immigration controls and that it was 'shameful for a modern democracy to allow such an institution to persist' and in evoking national shame he 'spoke to left wing critiques that reference the dark memory of German concentration camps' (Fassin, 2012, p. 364).

References

Agamben, G. (2005) *State of Exception*. Stanford, CA: Stanford University Press.

Agamben, G. (1998) *Homo Sacer: Sovereign Power and Bare Life*. Stanford, CA: Stanford University Press.

Agamben, G. (1996) 'Beyond human rights', in L. Virno and M. Hardt (eds) *Radical Thought in Italy: A Potential Politics*. Minneapolis, MN: University of Minnesota Press, p. 160.

Aas, K.F. (2011) '"Crimmigrant" bodies and bona fide travelers: Surveillance, citizenship and global governance'. *Theoretical Criminology*, 15(3), pp. 331–346.

Achebe, C. (1977) 'An image of Africa: Racism in Conrad's *Heart of Darkness*'. *Massachusetts Review* (18th edn).

Agerholm, H. (2016) 'Calais "Jungle": Court rejects plans to demolish refugee shops set up in camp'. *The Independent*. Accessed 30 November 2016 at: www.independent.co.uk/news/world/europe/calais-jungle-court-rejects-plans-demolish-refugee-shops-restaurants-kids-cafe-set-up-camp-a7187726.html.

Agier, M. (2016) *Borderlands: Towards an Anthropology of the Cosmopolitan* (tr) David Fernback (ed.). Cambridge: Polity Press.

Bass, J.D. (1998) 'Hearts of darkness and hot zones: The ideologeme of imperial contagion in recent accounts of viral outbreaks'. *Quarterly Journal of Speech*, 84(4), pp. 430–447.

Bauman, Z. (1995) 'The century of camps', in P. Beilharz (ed.) *The Bauman Reader*. Malden, MA and Oxford: Blackwell Publishing, pp. 230–280.

Blumenthal, P. and Rieger, J.M. (2017) 'This stunningly racist French novel is how Steve Bannon explains the world'. *Huffington Post*. Accessed 30 November 2016 at: www.huffingtonpost.com/entry/steve-bannon-camp-of-the-saints-immigration_us_58b75206e4b0284854b3dc03.

Boswell, C (2012) 'How information scarcity influences the policy agenda: Evidence from U.K. immigration policy'. *Governance*, 25(3), pp. 367–389.

Bosworth, M. (2012) 'Subjectivity and identity in detention: Punishment and society in a global age'. *Theoretical Criminology*, 16(2), pp. 123–140.

Bosworth, M. and Guild, M. (2008) 'Governing through migration control: Security and citizenship in Britain'. *British Journal of Criminology*, 48(6), pp.703–719.

Bracchi, P. (2009) 'Bloody siege of Calais: The violent new breed of migrants who will let nothing stop them coming to Britain'. *Mail Online*. Accessed 30 November 2016 at: www.dailymail.co.uk/news/article-1202009/Bloody-siege-Calais-The-violent-new-breed-migrants-let-stop-coming-Britain.html#ixzz3soO3P7BV.

Bulman, M. (2017a) 'Charities vow to continue giving food to refugees despite Calais Mayor's ban'. *The Independent*. Accessed 30 November 2016 at: www.independent.co.uk/news/world/europe/calais-refugees-food-ban-charities-to-continue-distribution-despite-mayor-a7610321.html.

Bulman, M. (2017b) '"Endemic police brutality": The appalling treatment of refugees in northern France'. *The Independent*, 24 April, p. 3. Accessed at: www.independent.co.uk/news/world/europe/refugees-calais-northern-france-police-brutality-daily-basis-unaccompanied-

Bulman, M. (2016) 'Human rights lawyers blocked from entering Calais Jungle during demolition under State of Emergency ban'. *The Independent*. Accessed 30 November 2016 at: www.independent.co.uk/news/world/europe/human-rights-lawyers-blocked-calais-jungle-demolition-refugees-state-emergency-french-authorities-a7386031.html.

Chrisafis, A. (2015) '"At night it's like a horror movie" – inside Calais' official shantytown'. *The Guardian*. Accessed 30 November 2016 at: www.theguardian.com/world/2015/apr/06/at-night-its-like-a-horror-movie-inside-calaiss-official-shanty-town.

Commission for Racial Equality (2007) Memorandum. Submitted Joint Committee on Human Rights – Written Evidence. London: House of Lords; House of Commons. *Accessed* 11 January 2018 at: https://publications.parliament.uk/pa/jt200607/jtselect/jtrights/81/81we01.htm.

Daily Mail Reporter (2009) 'Razed to the ground: Jungle migrant camp emptied after raid by Calais police (but will it stop asylum seekers flooding into Britain?' Accessed 30 November 2016 at: www.dailymail.co.uk/news/article-1214161/French-Jungle-razed-week-immigrants-told-You-England-anymore-Calais.html.

Dearden, L. (2017) 'French human rights "at tipping point" as state of emergency continues, says Amnesty International'. *The Independent*. Accessed 30 November 2016 at: www.independent.co.uk/news/world/europe/france-state-of-emergency-extended-latest-human-rights-law-isis-amnesty-international-report-a7595251.html.

Diken, B. and Lausten, C.B. (2005) *The Culture of Exception: Sociology Facing the Camp*. London and New York: Routledge.

Dove, M.R. (1992) 'The dialectical history of "jungle" in Pakistan: An examination of the relationship between nature and culture'. *Journal of Anthropological Research*, 48(3), pp. 231–253.

Drogoul, F. and Hanryon, S. (2016) 'What next for refugees after demolition of the Calais Jungle'. *British Medical Journal*, 355 (November), p. i6192.

Elden, S. (2006) 'Spaces of humanitarian exception'. *Geografiska Annaler, Series B: Human Geography*, 88(4), pp. 477–485.

Fassin, D. (2012) 'Compassion and repression: The moral economy of immigration policies in France'. *Cultural Anthropology*, 23(3), pp. 362–387.

Geddes, A. (2005) 'Getting the best of both worlds? Britain, the EU and migration policy'. *International Affairs*, 81(4), pp. 723–740.

Gilroy, P. (2004) *Between Camps: Nations, Cultures and the Allure of Race*. London and New York: Routledge.

Gregory, D. (2006) 'The black flag: Guantánamo Bay and the space of exception'. *Geografiska Annaler Series B Human Geography*, 88, pp. 405–427.

Gutteridge, N. (2017) 'French court overturns Calais mayor's ban on charities distributing food to migrants'. *Express Online*. Accessed 30 November 2016 at: www.express.co.uk/news/world/783436/Calais-migrants-French-court-overturns-Mayor-Bouchart-refugee-food-ban.

Harvey, D. (1973) *Social Justice and the City*. London: Edward Arnold.

Howarth, A. and Ibrahim, Y. (2012) 'Threat and suffering: The liminal space of "the Jungle"', in L. Andrews and H. Roberts (eds) *Liminal Landscapes: Travel, Experience and Spaces In-between*. London: Routledge, pp. 200–216.

Hughes, P. and Spooner, H. (2016) 'Refugee crisis: What asylum seekers in the Calais Jungle hope for in 2016'. *The Independent*. Accessed 30 November 2016 at: www.independent.co.uk/news/world/europe/refugee-crisis-what-asylum-seekers-in-the-calais-jungle-hope-for-in-2016-a6797831.html.

Ibrahim, Y. (2011) 'Constructing "the Jungle": Distance framing in the *Daily Mail*'. *International Journal of Media and Cultural Politics*, 7(3), pp. 315–331.

Ibrahim, Y. and Howarth, A. (2014) 'The non-human interest story: De-personalizing the migrant'. In *New Racisms: Forms of Un/Belonging in Britain Today*. Sussex Centre for Cultural Studies. Accessed at: http://bura.brunel.ac.uk/bitstream/2438/11653/2/Fulltext.pdf.

Ibrahim, Y. and Howarth, A. (2015) 'Space construction in media reporting: A study of the migrant space in the "Jungles" of Calais'. *Fast Capitalism*, 1(12). Accessed 11 January 2018 at: http://bura.brunel.ac.uk/handle/2438/11323.

Ibrahim, Y. and Howarth, A. (2017) 'Communicating the "migrant" other as risk: space, EU and expanding borders'. *Journal of Risk Research*. Accessed 17 April 2017 at: https://doi.org/10.1080/13669877.2017.1313765.

Isakjee, A., Davies, T. and Dhesi, S.K. (2015) *Independent Report into Conditions in Calais Migrant Camps Outlines Failure to Meet Recommended Standards*. Accessed 30 November 2016 at: www.birmingham.ac.uk/Documents/colleges/gees/research/calais-report-oct-2015.pdf.

Isin, E. and Rygiel, K. (2007) 'Of other global cities: Frontiers, zones, camps', in B. Drieskens, F. Mermier and H. Wimmen (eds) *Cities of the South: Citizenship and Exclusion in the 21st Century*. London: Saqi, pp. 170–209.

Johnston, P. (2009) 'The Calais jungle has been cleared – but this tide of despair has only just begun'. *The Telegraph*. Accessed 30 November 2016 at: www.telegraph.co.uk/comment/columnists/philipjohnston/6220076/The-Calais-jungle-has-been-cleared-but-this-tide-of-despair-has-only-just-begun.html.

Katz, I. (2015) 'From spaces of thanatopolitics to spaces of natality: A commentary on "Geographies of the camp"'. *Political Geography*, 49, pp. 84–86.

Kolosov, V. (2015) 'Geography of camps in the Stalin epoch: Experiences and lessons'. *Political Geography*, 49, pp. 87–89.

McGuiness, R. (2016) '"Go home now and GET £2.5K": Besieged France offers migrants WINDFALL to leave'. *Express Online*. Accessed 30 November 2016 at: www.express.co.uk/news/world/736081/france-offers-money-displaced-calais-jungle-migrants-return-home-payment-immigration.

Marrus, M.R. (1985) The Unwanted: European Refugees in the Twentieth Century. Oxford: Oxford University Press.

Millner, N. (2011) 'From "refugee" to "migrant" in Calais solidarity activism: Re-staging undocumented migration for a future politics of asylum'. *Political Geography*, 30, pp. 320–328.

Minca, C. (2005) 'Viewpoint: The return of the camp'. *Progress in Human Geography*, 29(4), pp 405–412.

Minca, C. (2015a) 'Counter-camps and other spatialities'. *Political Geography*, 49, pp. 90–92.

Minca, C. (2015b) 'Geographies of the camp'. *Political Geography*, 49, pp.74–83.

Mulvey, G. (2010) 'When policy creates politics: The problematizing of immigration and the consequences for refugee integration in the UK'. *Journal of Refugee Studies*, 23(4), pp. 437–462.

Netz, R. (2004) *Barbed Wire: An Ecology of Modernity*. Durham, NC: Wesleyan University Press.

Peake, A. (2008) 'Inside Jungle rape camp'. *The Sun*. Accessed 30 November 2016 at: www.thesun.co.uk/sol/homepage/features/1627718/Inside-Jungle-rape-camp.html.

Puggioni, R. (2006) 'Resisting sovereign power: Camps in-between exception and dissent', in J. Huysmans, A. Dobson and R. Prokhovnik (eds) *The Politics of Protection: Sites of Insecurity and Political Agency*. London and New York: Routledge, pp. 68–83.

Pugliese, J. (2002) 'Penal asylum: Refugees, ethics, hospitality'. *Borderlands*, 1(1). Accessed 30 November 2016 at: www.borderlands.net.au/vol1no1_2002/pugliese.html.

Ramadan, A. (2013) 'Spatialising the refugee camp'. *Transactions of the Institute of British Geographers*, 38(1), pp. 65–77.

Reid, S. (2016) 'Nowhere but Britain will do: The incredible 3,000-mile journey of the "laughing migrant" who was rescued from a dinghy in the Channel after vowing to smuggle his way into the UK'. *Daily Mail*. Accessed 30 November 2016 at: www.dailymail.co.uk/news/article-3995870/Nowhere-Britain-incredible-3-000-mile-journey-laughing-migrant-rescued-dinghy-Channel-vowing-smuggle-way-UK.html.

Rose, S. (2016) 'Why the "white man in the jungle" film won't die'. *The Guardian*. Accessed 30 November 2016 at: www.theguardian.com/film/2016/jul/06/why-the-white-man-in-the-jungle-film-wont-die.

Schwenken, H. (2014) 'From Sangatte to "The Jungle": Europe's contested border-lands', in H. Schwenken (ed.) *New Border and Citizenship Politics*. Basingstoke: Palgrave Macmillan, pp. 171–186.

Shields, R. (1999) 'Culture and the economy of cities'. *European Urban and Regional Studies*, 6(4), pp. 303–311.

Sinmaz, E. (2016) 'Child refugees from Jungle go missing'. *Daily Mail*. Accessed 30 November 2016 at: www.dailymail.co.uk/news/article-4023084/Child-refugees-Jungle-missing-Fears-trafficked-prostitution-slavery-disappearing-council-care.html.

Slater, D. (2004) 'For a post-colonial geopolitics', in D. Slater (ed.) *Geopolitics and the Post-Colonial: Rethinking North-South Relations*. Malden, MA and London: Blackwell.

Stoddart, T. (2006) 'A small girl looks through barbed wire at a refugee camp in Macedonia where thousands of Albanians were kept after being "ethnically cleansed" from their homes in Kosovo in 1999'. *Getty Images*. Accessed 30 November 2016 at: www.gettyimages.fi/detail/news-photo/news-photo/200392127-001#small-girl-looks-through-barbed-wire-at-a-refugee-camp-in-macedonia-picture-id200392127.

Stone, D. (2017) *Concentration Camps: A Short History*. Oxford: Oxford University Press.

Taylor, M., Topping, A., Domokos, J. and Mahmood, M. (2015) 'Fortress Calais: fleeting fixtures and precarious lives in the migrant camp', *The Guardian*. Accessed 30 November 2016 at: www.theguardian.com/world/2015/jul/27/migrant-camp-fortress-calais-jungle.

The Times (2016) 'Law of the Jungle'. Accessed 30 November 2016 at: www.thetimes.co.uk/article/law-of-the-jungle-kpzfvr7lr.

Thomas, D. (2013) *Into the European 'Jungle'*. Bloomington, IN: Indiana University Press.

Thorpe, J. (2011) 'Displacing empire: Refugee welfare, national activism and state legitimacy in Austria-Hungary in the First World War'. In P. Panayi and P. Virdee (eds) *Refugees and the End of Empire: Imperial Collapse and FORCED MIGRATion*. Basingstoke: Palgrave Macmillan, pp. 102–126.

Trudeau, D. (2006) 'Politics of belonging in the construction of landscapes: Place-making, boundary-drawing and exclusion' *Cultural Geographies*, 13(3), pp. 421–433.

Wainwright, O. (2016) 'We built this city: how the refugees of Calais became its architects'. *The Guardian*. Accessed 30 November 2016 at: www.theguardian.com/artanddesign/2016/jun/08/refugees-calais-jungle-camp-architecture-festival-barbican.

Zaretsky, R. (2015) 'A moat defensive'. *Foreign Policy (Blog)*. Accessed 30 November 2016 at: http://foreignpolicy.com/2015/07/31/a-moat-defensive-english-channel-separating-migrants-calais/.

Zaretsky, R. (2016) 'France's perpetual state of emergency'. *Foreign Policy (Blog)*. Accessed 30 November 2016 at: http://foreignpolicy.com/2016/07/16/frances-perpetual-state-of-emergency/.

3 Turning the refugee into the unwanted migrant

Introduction

This chapter explores the management of Calais and its dispossessed inhabitants through the lens of policymaking in the UK. The humanitarian crisis in Calais and the Mediterranean was largely reduced to a migration crisis in government discourses as it sought to distance itself from any obligation or responsibility to these refugees, depicting them as 'marauding' or 'swarming' migrants (Mortimer, 2015; Taylor, 2015). Through such constructions, the crisis could be defined in policy terms as a security or border issue that justified enhancing security to dispel these human invaders.

Britain's response to the situation in Calais since the turn of the millennium has been at best reticent and at worst ambivalent, prompted into action to address rising anti-immigration sentiment in the UK, particularly with regard to criticisms of the UK having a 'sieve' rather than a border to push back the greedy migrants (Bosworth, 2008). Their reticence, contrary to successive governments, is evident in their emphasis on prioritizing protection of property over that of people and the 'flow of business' over that of refugees (Schuster, 2003). Michel Foucault (1975 [1977]) in his account of the shifting patterns of crime in modernity has drawn attention to how the protection of property was a critical response of the middle classes to the growth in ownership, wealth and investment. The difference is that the refugees of Calais are not concerned per se with the theft of property but with escaping their liminal predicament in France, an intention constructed by politicians in criminal terms of bypass laws on border controls. Here, the seminal work by Reviel Netz (2004) on the industrial production of barbed wire and its contribution to capitalism is more relevant to our argument. Netz demonstrates how the invention of barbed wire was critical in controlling movement across space hence colonizing it. The emphasis on securitization meant that the government was disposed to treating the large visible numbers of the displaced as threats rather than recognizing a sustained policy to address forced migration or a review of Western interventions in Afghanistan or the Middle East. The British response to the crisis was to also periodically exert pressure on the

French authorities including imposing a de facto ban on semi-permanent shelters or encampments (Howarth and Ibrahim, 2012). The blanket ban on basic human (and animal) need for shelter was performed as a symbolic and communicative device to deter 'migrants' from moving into the Anglo-French border spaces and to convey the lack of empathy for their predicament.

The lack of a sustained policy to manage forced migration in Calais and the Mediterranean became emblematic in capturing the trauma and violence inscribed on the bodies of the displaced. These dispossessed bodies can be denied not just refuge but also basic human needs. The increased securitization of the borders and renewed fortification through razor wire revealed the psychology of safeguarding their policy position through this biotechnology. A biotechnology originally designed to control the movement of feral cattle on the plains of the American West (Netz, 2004) was rolled out in Calais to control the movement of refugees and euphemistically called 'security fencing' by ministers (Ibrahim and Howarth, 2017) whose actions effectively turned Calais into a fortress, as it had been in medieval times. Refugees whether outside of the razor wire and those who managed to gain entry into the UK became enmeshed in a politics of depletion. While basic amenities such as shelter were denied to them in Calais, those who gained entry to the UK became highly regulated and governed bodies where further detention or renewed scrutiny on financial support awaited them. Financial support for asylum seekers has been systematically eroded over the past 30 years, a pattern accelerated under the austerity policies instigated by the Conservative government after 2010 (Joint Committee on Human Rights, 2013).[1]

The official discourses about refugees in Calais constituting a border or immigration problem created a context in which certain policies appear to be a common sense approach and helped legitimize certain actions while circumscribing others (cf. Fischer, 2003). Historically rooted imaginings of Calais as a gateway and the channel as defence against invasion provided the justification for increased securitization. Similarly, the Eurotunnel as a passage for traffic and trade stood to compromise defence, particularly the shift to open borders inside the EU (Reinisch, 2015). In this context, the policy priority of successive governments has been to shore up fortifications on Britain's border and systematically seal the gaps through which illegitimate bodies may cross the Channel. Calais in particular posed a visible threat of making the authorities looking powerless. While irregular migration is usually hidden out of sight in closed areas of airports or detention centres, or made public through court hearings or asylum and deportation statistics (Boswell, 2012), Calais with its unsightly and burgeoning camps threw open its bowels highlighting the threat of irregular migration to the nation and to securing its borders.

This chapter, in tracing the shifts in British policy from disengagement to reluctant or sporadic engagement with successive crises in Calais since the mid-1990s, highlights the lack of a sustained policy towards forced migration.

The management of migrants and their human needs have consistently been presented as a French matter. Similarly, the authorities sought to shift the responsibility of illegal bodies and incursions in Eurotunnel and the port onto the owners of the properties, such as hauliers, freight companies, etc., through the imposition of fines for each stowaway apprehended in Britain (Schuster, 2003).

High profile publicity campaigns framed in terms of porous borders and waged through the media by Eurotunnel and the freight companies have repeatedly drawn a reluctant British government into some form of intervention in the crises of Calais (Schuster, 2003). Their belated and begrudging interventions since 2000 have consistently prioritized security and flows of trade, a policy stance increasingly criticized as one of moral deficit and a betrayal of the British 'tradition of humanitarianism' (David Miliband cf. Borger, 2015). British reticence to embrace a proactive response was in effect consistent with the British rationale for entering the European Community in the 1970s, highlighting the contradictions and tensions in that tradition.

Britain, Europe, and incoherent responses to refugee crises

England's long retreat from Europe after the French re-capture of Calais in 1558 and its turn back towards the continent from the 1960s with the loss of its colonies, driven by an economic imperative to find new markets, was explored in an earlier chapter (Wall, 2012). It highlights the UK's conflicted and complex relationship with Calais and the Channel, reconciling competing interests between gateway and defence, trade and security. The fear of invasion runs deep in the British psyche, evident in the sustained resistance to the construction of a tunnel that physically linked Britain to the continent while being drawn to the economic advantages of increased trade through a tunnel that materialized in the latter part of the twentieth century (Daddow, 2013).

Britain, driven by an economic imperative, joined the European Economic Community (EEC) in 1972. From the outset there was an undercurrent of Euroscepticism in Britain's membership, but it had yet to resonate widely with the voters. In the 1974 referendum two-thirds of the electorate voted to remain in Europe. By the 2016 referendum public sentiment towards Europe yielded a slight majority for Brexit. The perception that sovereign power was being ceded to unelected officials in Brussels, the loss of control over immigration due to new member states outside the EU and anxieties over the EU holding Britain back from negotiating new trade agreements around the world were seen as the reasons for Brexit. Britain still wanted free movement of capital and goods but not the free movement of people and this was not a principle other member states were willing to concede.

The shock of Brexit is still reverberating but Britain had begun extricating itself from the European 'project' three decades earlier through a series of opt-outs from major treaties preferring instead to reassert sovereignty in key areas.

Not only had the UK opted out of the single currency in the Maastricht Treaty (1992) but also from open borders and the free movement of capital, goods and people in the Schengen Agreement (1994). It subsequently opted out of the asylum and immigration protocols in the Treaty of Amsterdam (1997) but opted into measures that tightened security, sought to discourage asylum seekers and reinforce controls on the external borders of the EU. Britain wanted a highly selective membership of the EU that privileged trade and security while safeguarding sovereignty and this premised its approach to the border politics of Calais. Three years before the opening of Eurotunnel in 1994, a bilateral Anglo-French agreement established juxtaposed or joint controls on both sides of Channel, effectively moving Britain's external border with Europe and the Schengen area to France. While opting out on open borders, Britain retained Schengen protocols on Intelligence and on fingerprinting. Under the terms of the Schengen agreement French police were prohibited from checking documents on trains. After 4000 undocumented refugees and migrants arrived in Waterloo on Eurostar in the second half of 2000, Britain negotiated a series of bilateral agreements for pre-embarkation checks by train companies (Schuster, 2003). British law from 1987 also delegated some of the responsibility for border controls to carriers. During the Sangatte crisis, airlines were being fined £2000 for every passenger they carried into Britain that did not have proper documentation. The imposing of punitive fines on Eurotunnel and haulier companies were to become a key factor in corporate opposition to the camps of Calais. Britain had not only managed to move the governance of border controls offshore but had shifted some of the responsibility of policing the borders to companies who resented it.

Beyond neoliberal politics,[2] policy developments in Brussels and events thousands of miles away mediated the border politics of Calais. An influx of refugees fleeing conflict and repression from Iraq to Afghanistan in the 1990s prompted attempts in Brussels to fashion a common response, a 'Europeanisation of refugee policies' in the EU (Lavenex, 2001). By 1995, refugee families were visibly sleeping rough in the parks and open spaces of Calais (Varada Raj, 2006). In 1991 the European Commission had issued a Communication on the 'right to asylum' taking a stronger humanitarian position on refugees but this was largely ineffectual. As the humanitarian crisis in the Balkans escalated in the late 1990s and in the Mediterranean from 2014, the initial EU response was ad hoc and fragmented, floundering on the resistance of states to any further encroachment on their sovereign rights. As Marie-Benedicte Dembour (2015) argues in her exploration of 'when humans become migrants', the European Court of Human Rights has since its inception privileged the rights of the sovereign state to determine entry over those of the refugee in search of sanctuary. However, the scale of successive crisis of mass refugees and the reluctance of member states to accept refugees despite being signatories of international treaties on their treatment necessitated more imaginative solutions.

The European Commission, in its search for alternative solutions, mooted a 'burden sharing' or 'quota scheme' in which refugees would be distributed among states in the Balkans and the Mediterranean, with the UK opting out in both cases (Ibrahim and Howarth, 2017). In the 1990s, the EU was forced to look elsewhere for solutions to the unfolding humanitarian crisis and it turned to off-shore options to keep refugees away from Europe. Effectively, the policy strategy shifted from managing refugees within the borders of the EU, towards one of 'internalisation' (Lavenex, 2001) in which the EU worked with humanitarian organizations to address the causes of forced migration and to contain refugees within the region. UN peacekeepers and monitors were deployed to areas in the Balkans to create 'safe havens' to protect the vulnerable and targeted. The strategy failed and the credentials of the humanitarian organizations and countries that took part, including Britain, were severely tarnished.

As the concerns about the Balkan refugees subsided, new ones emerged around internal immigration in the ever-expanding EU (Ibrahim and Howarth, 2016). Heightened tensions in Britain over internal migration from within the EU coincided with an escalating 'sense of chaos' at Europe's external borders as the crisis in North Africa and the Mediterranean unfolded from 2012. In an echo of the 'internalization' approach adopted during the Balkans crisis, Britain's initial response to the crisis was to be generous with humanitarian aid to Syria's neighbours and the UN becoming the second biggest bilateral donor to the region rather than accept Syrian refugees for resettlement within its borders. The rationale was to keep refugees as close to their homes as was safely possible so that when conflict ceased they could more readily return to their country of origin, in effect keeping them away from Britain's border in Calais.

The strategy was not entirely sustainable. As the crisis on its southern borders escalated, existing EU policies on refugees was 'tested' and internal divisions in the EU deepened as frontline states called for a re-allocating of responsibilities (Papademetriou, 2015). In 2014, Britain had successfully

Figure 3.1 Three boats with refugees are [sic] arriving at the beaches of Skala Sykamia, Lesvos, Greece

argued for the disbanding of the Mare Nostrum search-and-rescue scheme set up a year earlier by Italy to prevent more drownings, claiming that it would incentivize others to make the perilous journey across the Mediterranean (Figure 3.1). By 2015, with the crisis spiralling out of control and the front-line states overwhelmed by the number of refugees crossing their borders, the EU revived the idea floated during the Balkans crisis of a quota scheme in which refugees would be distributed between member states. Britain refused, arguing that the resettlement of any 'migrants' already in the EU would incentivize new waves of migration (see Boyle, 2017). The more rational response, they argued, was the militarization of the Mediterranean and the breaking up of the smuggling gangs that facilitated the influx of refugees. In support of the hard-line stance, Britain sent Royal Navy ships to the Mediterranean to work with Frontex, the agency set up to advise EU countries on border controls in 1999, to disrupt the smuggling rings.

After images of Alan Kurdi's body went viral in 2015, British public opinion on the response to the crisis polarized sharply between those in support of the government's 'hard-line approach' and those that argued for a humanitarian response. Claims about a moral responsibility to discourage the risky behaviour of 'migrants' smuggled across the Mediterranean were becoming politically damaging for Britain's international reputation. Stung by accusations that he was indifferent to suffering and that his policies were a betrayal of the British 'tradition of humanitarianism' (Borger, 2015), Cameron agreed to allow safe passage for 20,000 Syrian refugees in the UN camps of North Africa into Britain under its Vulnerable Persons Scheme (cf. Ibrahim and Howarth, 2017).[3] The scheme effectively externalized Britain's risk assessments. Entry required a double vetting, first by the UN to ascertain that they were 'genuine' refugees, then by the Home Office to determine what if any terrorist threat they may pose.

The plight of the child victims of war also became increasingly politicized with even the more right-wing British media calling for a partial relaxation of the policy stance to accommodate these most vulnerable of refugees. Again, Britain externalized its response, committing to the resettlement of 3000 vulnerable children (and family members) from conflict areas of the Middle East and North Africa. Externalizing of aid failed to appease critics including UNICEF, aid groups and some media which drew attention to the plight of the unaccompanied children already in the EU, particularly in Calais, and the perceived inadequacy of the government response. Faced with a parliamentary defeat as some of its own MPs backed the so-called 'Dubs Amendment', the government conceded and under section 67 of the Immigration Act 2016 agreed to relocate and support an unspecified number of unaccompanied children already in Europe. The Dubs Amendment was a rare concession. The Government's strategy and priority throughout the crisis continued to be the external vetting and processing of asylum applications.

Turning the refugee into the migrant

The labelling of the displaced as refugee or migrant become part of a wider political and ideological project in the UK. These provided subliminal and at times explicit justifications of who is worthy of sanctuary and who is trying to deplete the coffers of the nation. These labels as a deliberate discursive device enabled the government to build distance from the moral responsibility of acting to alleviate suffering (Ibrahim and Howarth, 2017). There emerges a cartography in ministers' discourse in the labels they employ towards the displaced. A 'refugee' in the UN camps in North Africa may be re-labelled as a 'migrant' when the entity crosses the Mediterranean (Figure 3.2).

The migrant becomes an economic opportunist rather than a persecuted individual fleeing for their lives. The word 'clandestines' has been employed in French and British policy discourses. A highly pejorative term, clandestine is more commonly used in France than Britain however, technically speaking, it only applies to people who attempt to bypass border controls and enter or leave the Schengen area illicitly (Fassin, 2012). Within the area, they can travel freely so their movement is no longer clandestine. Once in Calais, ministers tend to ascribe the label 'illegal migrant' for the same body that in the UN camps was deemed to be a refugee. Ascribing an illegality

Figure 3.2 View of the north coast of Lesbos between the villages of Molivos and Sykaminia. The coastal strip is full of lifejackets and refugee boats

Source: By Rosa-Maria Rinkl. September 2015. © BY-SA 4.0 International licence.

to their presence in Calais, de-legitimizes the camp's inhabitants, recasting them as criminals and threats, not only to the border but also to the established order of a civilized world. Legally the inhabitants of the camps are not refugees until they have applied for asylum and the status is conferred on them by a public body. The labelling of the camp migrants as illegal entities reasserts the power and right of the state to determine the status of those seeking sanctuary. However, most of those who passed through Sangatte, according to the UN were refugees 'stricto sensu' in that they fled their country of origin to escape danger (Fassin, 2012) and the same was said by NGOs about the inhabitants of the jungles (Bulman, 2016; Fassin, 2012).

In severing displaced bodies from the context of their forced displacement and recasting refugees as migrants, ministers have presented them as less deserving of our pity or compassion and presaging a retreat from the moral obligation to provide sanctuary. Ministers and media, in evoking the scale of the crisis, also evoked a fear of a 'migrant invasion' as a legitimate reason to harden the borders and prevent further incursions (Sheldrick, 2015). Zygmunt Bauman (2016) asserts that the term migration crisis is a 'codename' for the struggle for public sentiment and opinion, where the meaning is vague and alarmist, evoking fear rather than pity and a violent response that seeks to repel, obstruct or expel while presenting these as rational. Rather than hospitality, the desperate search for sanctuary has been met with force, the flight from violent persecution met with abrasive biotechnologies of razor wire and moats that not only obstruct movement but gouge, break or drown bodies of the most vulnerable, particularly children seeking sanctuary from persecution, police harassment and brutality (Bulman, 2017).

The responses of governments including Britain to the contemporary crisis have created a cognitive dissonance (Festinger, 1957, cf. Bauman, 2016) between their actions and the unconditional moral obligation to provide sanctuary. Bauman draws attention to how states have negotiated the dissonance by defaming the refugee (2016). In recasting them as migrants rather than refugees, the implication is that they are in Calais because of individual choice, free will and opportunism rather than being forcibly displaced or fleeing for their lives. The refugee has been presented as the object of fear, depersonalized in a numerical weight of numbers that threaten to overwhelm the 'thin blue line' of police in Calais and folded into a 'flood' that will destabilize Britain and her coffers. If hard borders are not shored up, British culture, standards of living and civilization will be at risk of being overwhelmed. The figure of the refugee is at once denigrated and dehumanized where discourses of 'marauding' or 'swarming' frame them through a primal tribalism congruent with those from the jungle. Even for the children, 'feral' (Gilligan, 2016) entities conjoined them with the barbarism of the jungle, denying them humanity and the need for protection. The circulation of these virulent discourses in the public sphere not only shapes public sentiment and attitudes to immigration against the context of austerity, but also circumscribes what policy actions are possible, justifying and legitimizing certain enactments over others. Bauman (2016) concludes the crisis facing Europe is one of 'humanity' and not migration.

From Sangatte to the Jungles

Refugees fleeing conflict and persecution in the Balkans, Afghanistan and Iraq began appearing in Calais from the mid-1990s. The French government in 1999 requisitioned a hangar in Sangatte from Eurotunnel and asked the Red Cross to open a temporary shelter to provide basic amenities including shelter, food, showers and toilets. The justification given was a mix of humanitarian and public order but the sight of families with children sleeping rough in Calais had been an embarrassment to the French authorities. Sangatte gave the authorities the opportunity to 'tidy people away' but also have their basic needs met (Schuster, 2003). Provided that the temporary occupants of the Centre were able to move on into Britain or elsewhere there were few problems, but repeated incursions into the port and the tunnel areas prompted the companies to tighten security. As onward movement across the Channel became increasingly restricted, more refugees began to arrive. By the time of its closure in 2002, more than 65,000 Kosovans, Iraqis and Afghans had passed through (Liagre and Dumont, 2005; Schuster, 2003). The shelter had become synonymous in much of British political discourse with overcrowding, inter-ethnic violence, rioting as well as unbearable squalor, noise and stench. For the next five years until the jungle replaced it, Sangatte was held up by British ministers and media as a salutary lesson on what to avoid in Calais. Any suggestion mooted by charities or more left-leaning French politicians for government-supported humanitarian measures in the form of semi-permanent structures to serve as shelters or ablution blocks for refugees in Calais was labelled by some British politicians and media as potential 'mini-Sangattes' (Varada Raj, 2006). A policy response of active discouragement and deterrence took precedence over one of humanitarian relief.

The evoking of the spectre of Sangatte by British politicians and media is not without irony. In the late 1990s, the British government was unwilling to get involved in the burgeoning refugee crisis in Calais and saw no need to. The country's external border was offshore and the Channel created a natural barrier. Ministers perceived the 'management of migrants' on French soil to be a French matter, humanitarian need was for charities to respond to and disruptions to Eurotunnel and the port caused by incursions was a matter for the companies whose property was being trespassed on (Schuster, 2002). With its active displacement of responsibilities or ownership of the issues, government's only concern was if and when 'illegal migrants' reached British shores. Under the carrier laws first introduced in 1987, it fined companies for failing to detect stowaways (Schuster, 2003). The policy approach adopted by Britain to border politics was one of devolution and delegation of responsibility. However, by 2002 the intense media and policy campaigns of the companies had begun to pay off, Home Secretary David Blunkett was lobbying for the closure of Sangatte and a year later Britain agreed in the Le Touquet treaty to contribute to the security of the port (BBC News, 2003; Geddes, 2005). Not content with restricting access to welfare support for basic needs in Britain, the government also effectively lobbied their French counterparts to impose a de facto ban on any semi-permanent shelters that lasted until 2015 when the Calais authorities felt compelled to open the Jules Ferry overnight shelter for women and children to protect them from rape. The same argument used to justify the closure of Sangatte was used by successive ministers in lobbying for the demolition of Jungle 1 in 2009 and Jungle 2 in 2016, i.e. informal camps served as a 'magnet for migrants' and provided hiding places for criminals including people smugglers (Ibrahim and Howarth, 2014). Not only denied basic shelter, the movement of refugees and migrants in Calais was increasingly curtailed. In 2014, Prime Minister David Cameron pledged £12 million to defend Eurotunnel and the port after repeated mass attempts to board trains and ferries had brought transport to a standstill. Razor wire was also extended along the access routes to the port and tunnel and in 2016 after Jungle 2 had been demolished, work was completed on a wall along the routes. Medieval fortifications around Calais captured in Hogarth's painting and pulverized during two world wars had been rebuilt with substantial investment from Britain. The fortifications this time were not intended to defend the town but to restrict access to the gateways across the Channel, prevent onward movement of the unwanted and ensure the flow of commerce. Over 15 years, Britain's policy position had shifted from disinterested bystander to begrudging yet selective engagement that privileged a neoliberal agenda of trade.

The policy shift was not in response to repeated humanitarian crises on Britain's front doorstep but to an orchestrated campaign and lobbying by the companies most affected by refugee attempts to stow across the Channel. Eurotunnel and the port authorities responded to repeated incursions by tightening security around the perimeter of their properties. Notwithstanding a £2 million investment in security, Eurotunnel encountered a major incursion in December 2001 that brought trains to a standstill over Christmas (Schuster, 2003). Not only did they have to deal with the financial consequences of an interruption to business, the companies were also fined £2000 for each undocumented passenger they brought into Britain. In a precursor of their responses to the 2015 disruption, the Rail Freight Association called for the army to be sent in with razor wire to secure the tunnel. The closure of Sangatte became an 'imperative' for Eurotunnel who perceived the camp as a 'direct threat' to business and the fines imposed by the British courts as iniquitous when the French police rounded up trespassers, took them back to Sangatte where they were then free to try again the next night (Schuster, 2003).

The respective governments on both sides of the Channel were initially indifferent to lobbying by Eurotunnel, prompting it to unsuccessfully apply to the French courts to close Sangatte, challenge the fines in the British courts and wage a highly effective media campaign. Eurotunnel invited television crews and photojournalists onto its property to capture and distribute images of refugees cutting and scaling fences, scrambling down embankments and running along railway tracks. Similar dramatic imaging of incursions on a much larger scale was repeated in the summer of 2015 during the ferry workers strike and with more violent clashes between the police and refugees. Eurotunnel's media campaign resonated precisely because it presented the feat of engineering as a risk, tapping into long held fears of any compromising of the protective moat offered by the English Channel (cf. Boswell 2012). Discourses which presented Sangatte as a 'magnet' for migrants and a 'gathering space for buyers and sellers' where deals could be struck with people traffickers and individual truckers willing to risk taking stowaways across (Schuster, 2003) tapped into latent fears of invasion by the criminal Other. These discourses were later appropriated in ministerial justifications which reconfigured the demolition of the jungle as a magnanimous act of rooting out the criminal networks that preyed on the vulnerable, a humanitarian act rather than a violent one (see Bracchi, 2009).

However, the shift in policy position from disinterested bystander to reluctant, selective engagement required a shift in ministerial personnel on both sides of the Channel. Home Secretary Jack Straw took the view that if carriers did not want to pay fines they needed to improve their security (Schuster, 2003). His successor David Blunkett found himself grappling with shifting public sentiment that coincided with a decade long anti-immigration campaign in the media that peaked in 2003. Despite a raft of immigration-related legislation over three decades, the public perception was that the Government had lost control of its borders and that asylum policy was in crisis (Mulvey, 2010). A surge in asylum figures appeared to confirm that and media images of refugees walking through the tunnel at night appeared to provide visual evidence to support the statistics. Blunkett pledged to lobby his French counterparts and in 2002 the newly appointed Interior Minister Nicolas Sarkozy agreed to close Sangatte. Rising anti-immigrant sentiment had turned Calais into a stronghold for the National Front but almost immediately after it closed, 'mini-Sangattes' or 'jungles' sprung up, each one a new symbol of the failure of British and French policies, but together they provided a composite of the lack of political will over time to devise a sustainable strategy to the ongoing policy problem of refugees in Calais.

The economic imperative that had drawn Britain back to Europe continued to shape its policy approaches to Calais. Security and flows of business trade remained the priority of successive governments but that is not to say ministers did not at times engage with the human dimensions. The plight of the human however became a lever in bilateral agreements and arrangements in 2003 and 2016. In exchange for the closure of the camp, Britain agreed to take a proportion of the occupants of Sangatte; the rest were dispersed to reception centres around France or repatriated to their country of origin (*The Telegraph*, 2002). In 2009, the government refused to take any of the children displaced by the demolition of the Jungle; however, under the so-called 'Dubs Amendment' in the 2016 Immigration Act the government agreed to relocate an unspecified number of unaccompanied children from the camp. The government of Theresa May consistently resisted any other attempt to open a legal route into Britain for undocumented refugees and migrants (May, 2016).

Britain's legislative retreat from humanitarianism

The lack of a coherent approach and the constant shifts in policy to assuage public sentiments, and in tandem the need to appear in touch with concerns over uncontrolled immigration, also brought a fair share of criticism against the government from left-wing media, opposition politicians and religious leaders for being at odds with Britain's 'tradition' of humanitarian treatment of refugees particularly the provision of sanctuary or asylum to the persecuted.[4] The obligation to provide protection for the beleaguered and sanctuary is deeply rooted in ancient Judaeo-Christian mythology and Enlightenment thinking that has been incorporated into international treaties on the treatment of refugees (Kleingeld, 1998). However, the tradition is more conflicted and fractured than critics acknowledge, particularly in operational terms.

The origins of the tradition of sanctuary can traced to the Huguenots fleeing religious persecution and by the nineteenth century the provision of refuge had evolved into a heightened sense of British exceptionalism and moral superiority (cf. Shaw, 2015). The nation, it was believed, differed not only in their island status but also because they were one of the last of the European states to reinstate border controls with the 1905 Aliens Act and equally the reluctance of successive governments to deport or extradite nationalists or revolutionaries championing the historic ideal of sanctuary. By the Victorian era, the sense of this distinctive tradition of asylum had become part of a powerful social imaginary and national identity (Shaw, 2015). Critics of Britain's response to the contemporary crisis in the Mediterranean have evoked the nostalgic history of Save the Children, a British NGO set up after the First World War with the purpose of feeding children starving in Europe after the Allied blockade (cf. Helm, 2016). The Kindertransport scheme that rescued thousands of Jewish children from Nazi-controlled Europe has been evoked as a rebuke to the Cameron–May apparent indifference to the plight of unaccompanied child refugees in Calais (Janner-Klausner, 2015).

The notion of a distinctive tradition of sanctuary and international moral leadership is more myth than reality. Unlike its European counterparts, Victorian Britain did not distinguish between nationality, creed or political orientation in allowing exiles to remain. The distinction was perceived to be an epitome of liberal enlightened thinking and informed a sense of moral superiority. Fissures in the myth were exposed though with mass forced migration beginning with the Ashkenazi Jews in the 1880s. The 1905 Aliens Act which reinstated border controls after a hiatus of 140 years also reasserted sovereign power to determine not only who may stay but also who many enter. The febrile debates leading up to the Act were highly polarized between a visceral anti-Semitism and the view of high profile figures such as Winston Churchill who believed elements of the Bill betrayed the distinctive British tradition of refuge. The compromise agreed was to introduce asylum as a legal category but exclude the destitute, diseased and criminal from the right to asylum with the ultimate decision being a matter of ministerial discretion. Although the face of the Act was not as explicitly xenophobic as subsequent legislation, the exclusions have been widely interpreted as a code for Anti-Semitism and set a racialized tone for subsequent legislation in the latter part of the century. With the advent of war in 1914 and again in 1939 the right to asylum was suspended and many who fled to Britain from Nazi-occupied Europe including the Calais prefecture of Vichy France were sent back to their deaths.

Post-war, while Britain played a leading role in protecting the rights of refugees in international law, the situation was more ambivalent than popular imagination suggests. British lawyers played a role in drafting international treaties, but successive governments were more conservative about who those rights should apply to. The first international conventions were Euro-centric and refugee rights were restricted to those displaced in Europe by the Second World War, and subsequent attempts to universalize the definition of a refugee to include anyone fleeing persecution anywhere were unsuccessfully resisted by British ministers. The international initiatives coincided with de-colonization and instability and ministers feared that universalizing the concept and rights would create an expectation that Britain would grant refuge to those fleeing persecution in former colonies or the Commonwealth.

Britain sought to tighten its domestic legislation as a means to restrict entry. The retreat from the ideal that had started with the 1905 Aliens Act accelerated after the 1970s. Not only were border controls tightened, ministers assumed more power and a greater willingness to deport those deemed to be undesirables. Racial delineations intensified. Britain allowed in Asians expelled in the post-liberation Uganda but, afraid of an influx from other African states, reneged on a promise and denied Kenyan Asians entry. Thousands unwanted in Kenya and unable to gain sanctuary in Britain or India, found themselves stateless for the next three decades.

Thereafter racial delineation in legislation strengthened. Commonwealth citizens were denied automatic right to entry and the introduction of patrial criteria further racialized who was allowed in. In addition, ministers were increasingly willing to exercise their discretion and visas became an instrument of power to control the influx of refugees from unstable and failed states. At the same time that British NGOs were expanding in size and global reach, the opportunities to secure sanctuary were contracting and the rights of refugees in Britain steadily being diluted. Those forced to flee for their lives in search of sanctuary were increasingly dependent on people traffickers and smugglers.

Those that made it into Britain encountered further tensions between practice and ideal, particularly in accessing public funds. The contradictions are not new, they date back to the Huguenots when anyone in principle had access to poor relief. In practice, refugees or exiles often found their way obstructed by religious officials who feared a depletion of limited resources or encountered hostility from locals who perceived them as competing for jobs. For over 400 years, refugees who found sanctuary in Britain were often reduced to penury. The 1905 Act excluded the right of the 'destitute' to asylum, refusing refuge to Ashkenazi Jews who had lost everything in their flight from Russian pogroms and the debates then and now often centre on competition for access to limited public resources including schools and housing.

The 1905 Act created a legal category of asylum and a precedent in which ministerial power to determine the right to sanctuary was based not on the reasons why they fled but whether those who sought help were seen as a threat to resources or policy. Between 1933 and 1938 Jewish refugees had to demonstrate independent support or sponsorship and commit to leave after the cessation of hostilities (i.e. prove they would not be a drain). More recently, in the blame-game played out in Calais, the common French accusation is that over-generous British benefits are a 'magnet for migrants', a discourse that resonates as powerfully now as similar ones did during debates on the 1905 Act yet is contradicted by the steady contraction of financial support in Britain for asylum seekers (Mulvey, 2010).

Such discourses have justified a series of laws, particularly in austerity Britain, intended to create a 'hostile' environment for asylum seekers, many of whom are reduced to abject poverty. Nowhere has the parsimoniousness of British governments been more evident than in the implementation of the Dubs Amendment in the 2016 Immigration Act that committed to the rescue of unaccompanied children from the jungles in Calais. The number was left to ministerial discretion and as a growing number of unaccompanied children began stowing away into Britain, councils particularly on the east coast appealed to the government for more financial support to help support them. The government instead chose to disperse the children around the councils and by the time the scheme was quietly closed in early 2017 only 350 had been brought in, 750 less than envisaged by the Cameron government and a fraction of the 3000 that Save the Children had called for.

Conclusion

The UK government's approach to Calais needs to be historically contextualized. Since the Aliens Act in 1905 there has been a conflicted policy towards those seeking sanctuary. On the one hand, the UK straddles a romantic illusory of being a safe haven for the dispossessed. Over time, through its relationship with the wider world encompassing colonization, its policy of regionalism with the EU and withdrawal of responsibility from the former colonies, the 'refugee' is assessed through tightening policies and visceral politics that are increasingly reticent and weary of the vulnerable 'Other'. The policy towards Calais has been one of displacement. The constant skirmishes with the French and the need to look decisive to the British public anxious about Britain opening its borders and coffers has infused a policy that is often reactive and conceived through a short-term vision. Most importantly, it is premised on placing the onus on its European neighbours and external off-shore entities to manage. The politics of displacement with Calais and the foisting of it as a problem for others to attend to means that Calais and the camps have been reduced to a nexus of securitization and border control, needing periodic material and symbolic acts of expiation to dispel the camps and to appropriate a hard line of zero tolerance to shelters through denial of basic amenities. The shifting terminology between a 'migrant' and a 'refugee' has become an instrumental device to ascribe violence, criminality and the lack of responsibility to bodies (both dead and alive) hoping to cross the UK border.

Notes

1 In 1996, the British government took refugee financial support out of the welfare system. Responsibility for determining who received financial support, how much, for how long and what terms fell under the auspices of the Home Office. That is, financial support of asylum seekers was reconstituted as an immigration rather than a welfare issue. There was also growing criticism especially from NGOs which argued that the government intention was to "starve" refugees out of Britain (cf. Mulvey 2010).

2 While 'neoliberal' can be an amorphous term, we are using it to refer to a political ideology predicated on the belief that government interventions should be restricted to law, order and the safeguarding of trade and commerce.

3 The Syrian Vulnerable Person Resettlement Programme (VPRP) at first prioritized the elderly, the disabled and the victims of sexual violence and torture. Initially, resettled Syrians were given 'humanitarian protection' status for five years with permission to work and access public funds. In March 2017, the Home Secretary acknowledged that the status did not carry the same entitlements as

those under refugee status and announced all those granted humanitarian protection would be given refugee status. By March 2017, 5453 instead of the estimated 20,000 had been resettled under the scheme (McGuinness, 2017).

4 The notion of sanctuary is an ancient one. In classical and Judeao-Christian traditions, there was a moral expectation that sanctuary or refuge would be offered on sacred sites to slaves, fugitives and exiles who had fled in fear for their lives. The imperative to provide sanctuary was driven by a fear of the vengeance of God/gods. Sanctuary, codified first under the Holy Roman Empire then under the Papacy, lasted for over 1000 years and became one of the most important and powerful medieval institutions. It was only with the secularization of society, that responsibility for the provision of sanctuary passed from the religious orders to the state. Between the 17th and 19th centuries, sanctuary practices began to fragment as states became more willing to extradite exiles because of their religious or political beliefs. The exception was Britain which during the Victorian era gained a reputation as a provider of humanitarian refuge irrespective of belief. It was in this period that a particular imagining of a distinctively British "tradition" of humanitarian refuge began to emerge. However, with the 1905 Aliens Act and the reinstatement of border controls this 'tradition' began to erode (cf. Ibrahim and Howarth, 2017a).

References

Bauman, Z. (2016) *Strangers at Our Door*. Cambridge: Polity Press.

BBC News (2003) 'UK discussing UN asylum obligations', 5 February. Accessed 30 November 2016 at: http://news.bbc.co.uk/1/hi/uk_politics/2723345.stm.

Borger, J. (2015) 'David Miliband: Failure to take in refugees an abandonment of UK's humanitarian traditions'. *The Guardian*, 2 September. Accessed 30 November 2016 at: www.theguardian.com/world/2015/sep/02/david-miliband-refugees-uk-humanitarian-traditions.

Boswell, C. (2012) 'How information scarcity influences the policy agenda: Evidence from UK immigration policy'. *Governance*, 25(3), pp. 367–389.

Bosworth, M. (2008) 'Border control and the limits of the sovereign state'. *Social and Legal Studies*, 17(2), pp. 199–215.

Boyle, F. (2015) 'Cameron won't take refugees who have reached Europe – like there's a humanitarian offside rule'. *Guardian*. 14 September. Accessed 11 January 2018 at: www.theguardian.com/commentisfree/2015/sep/14/cameron-refugees-europe-humanitarian-british-government-migrants-camps-frankie-boyle.

Bracchi, P. (2009) 'Bloody siege of Calais: The violent new breed of migrants who will let nothing stop them coming to Britain'. *MailOnline*, 25 July. Accessed 30 November 2016 at: www.dailymail.co.uk/news/article-1202009/Bloody-siege-Calais-The-violent-new-breed-migrants-let-stop-coming-Britain.html.

Bulman, M. (2016) 'France blocks lawyers from helping Jungle refugees'. *The Independent*, 31 October. Accessed 30 November 2016 at: www.independent.co.uk/news/world/europe/human-rights-lawyers-blocked-calais-jungle-demolition-refugees-state-emergency-french-authorities-a7386031.html.

Bulman, M. (2017) '"Endemic police brutality": The appalling treatment of refugees in northern France'. *The Independent*, 24 April. Accessed 30 November 2016 at: www.independent.co.uk/news/world/europe/refugees-calais-northern-france-police-brutality-daily-basis-unaccompanied-minors-children-a7696076.html.

Daddow, O. (2013) 'Margaret Thatcher, Tony Blair and the Eurosceptic tradition in Britain'. *British Journal of Politics and International Relations*, 15(2), pp. 210–227.

Dembour, M-B. (2015) *When Humans Become Migrants: Study of the European Court of Human Rights with an Inter-American Counterpoint*. Oxford: Oxford University Press.

Fassin, D. (2012) 'Compassion and repression: The moral economy of immigration policies in France'. *Cultural Anthropology*, 23(3), pp. 362–387.

Fischer, F. (2003) *Reframing Public Policy: Discursive Politics and Deliberative Practices*. Oxford: Oxford University Press.

Foucault, M. (1977) *Discipline and punish: the birth of the prison.* Tr. A. Sheridan. New York: Random House

Geddes, A. (2005) 'Getting the best of both worlds? Britain , the EU and migration policy'. *International Affairs*, 81(4), pp. 723–740.

Gilligan, A. (2016) 'UK's child refugees vanish', *The Sunday Times*, 11 December. Accessed 30 November 2016 at: www.thetimes.co.uk/article/uks-child-refugees-vanish-q6xxrt706.

Helm, T. (2016) 'Pressure grows on Theresa May to admit 3,000 lone refugee children to UK', *The Observer*, 16 January. Accessed 30 November 2016 at: www.theguardian.com/global-development/2016/jan/16/pressure-grows-on-theresa-may-to-admit-3000-lone-refugee-children-to-uk.

Howarth, A. and Ibrahim, Y. (2012) 'Threat and suffering: The liminal space of "the Jungle"', in L. Andrews and H. Roberts (eds) *Liminal Landscapes: Travel, Experience and Spaces In-between*. London: Routledge, pp. 200–216.

Ibrahim, Y. and Howarth, A. (2014) 'The non-human interest story: De-personalizing the migrant', in *New Racisms: Forms of Un/Belonging in Britain Today*. Sussex Centre for Cultural Studies.

Ibrahim, Y. and Howarth, A. (2016) 'Constructing the Eastern European Other: The horsemeat scandal and the migrant Other'. *Journal of Contemporary European Studies*, 2804 (February), pp. 1–17.

Ibrahim, Y. and Howarth, A. (2017) 'Communicating the "migrant" Other as risk: Space, EU and expanding borders'. *Journal of Risk Research*, published online 17 April. Accessed 11 January 2018 at: www.tandfonline.com/doi/abs/10.1080/13669877.2017.1313765?journalCode=rjrr20.

Janner-Klausner, L. (2015) 'When Jewish people look at Calais migrants, we see ourselves'. *The Guardian*, 13 August. Accessed 30 November 2016 at: www.theguardian.com/commentisfree/2015/aug/13/jewish-people-calais-migrants-kindertransport-children-nazis.

Joint Committee on Human Rights (2013) 'Human rights of unaccompanied migrant children and young people in the UK', 12 June. Accessed 30 November 2016 at: www.publications.parliament.uk/pa/jt201314/jtselect/jtrights/9/9.pdf.

Kleingeld, P. (1998) 'Kant's Cosmopolitan Law: World citizenship for a global order', *Kantian Review*, 2, pp. 72–90.

Lavenex, S. (2001) *Revival: The Europeanisation of Refugee Policies: Between Human Rights and Security*. London and New York: Routledge.

Liagre, R. and Dumont, F. (2005) 'Sangatte: Life and death of a refugee center'. *Annales de Geographie*, 1(641), pp. 92–112.

McGuinness, R. (2017) 'Calais Jungle RETURNS: Officials say it's LAWLESS AND DANGEROUS and deem it a "NO-GO ZONE"'. *Express Online*, 19 January. Accessed 30 November 2016 at: www.express.co.uk/news/world/756356/Calais-Jungle-returns-lawless-dangerous-no-go-zone-France-refugee-camp.

May, T. (2016) *House of Commons Debate: Migration (Africa to the EU)*. 11 April. Accessed 30 November 2016 at: www.theyworkforyou.com/debates/?id=2016-04-11a.1.3&s=calais+speaker%3A10426+speaker%3A10426+speaker%3A10426#g1.7.

Mortimer, C. (2015) 'Philip Hammond's demonisation of "marauding" migrants is shameful, says Amnesty International'. *The Independent*, 10 August, p. 10447901. Accessed 30 November 2016 at: www.independent.co.uk/news/uk/politics/philip-hammonds-demonising-of-marauding-migrants-comments-is-shameful-10447901.html.

Mulvey, G. (2010) 'When policy creates politics: the problematizing of immigration and the consequences for refugee integration in the UK', *Journal of Refugee Studies*, 23(4), pp. 437–462.

Netz, R. (2004) *Barbed Wire: An Ecology of Modernity*. Durham, NC: Wesleyan University Press.

Papademetrious, D. (2015) 'Migration crisis tests European consensus and governance'. *Migration Policy Institute*. 18 December. Accessed at: www.migrationpolicy.org/article/top-10-2015-issue-1-migration-crisis-tests-european-consensus-and-governance.

Reinisch, J. (2015) '"Forever temporary": Migrants in Calais, then and now'. *Political Quarterly*, 86(4), pp. 515–522.

Schuster, L. (2002) 'Sangatte: A false crisis'. *Global Dialogue: Nicosia*, 4(4), pp. 57–68.

Schuster, L. (2003) 'Asylum seekers: Sangatte and the Tunnel'. *Parliamentary Affairs*, 56(3), p. 506–522+ii+v.

Shaw, C. (2015) *Britannia's Embrace: Modern Humanitarianism and the Imperial Origins of Refugee Relief*. Oxford: Oxford University Press.

Sheldrick, G. (2015) 'Calais migrant crisis: Sangatte never produced scenes like this, say tunnel bosses'. *The Express*, 30 July. Accessed 30 November 2016 at: www.express.co.uk/news/uk/595050/Calais-migrants-Sangatte-eurotunnel

Slack, J. (2015) 'The marauding migrants from Africa threaten our standard of living, says Philip Hammond'. *Mail Online*, 10 August. Accessed 30 November 2016 at: www.dailymail.co.uk/news/article-3191665/The-marauding-migrants-Africa-threaten-standard-living-says-Philip-Hammond-.

Taylor, M. (2015) 'Calais crisis: "It's easier to leave us living like this if you say we are bad people"; Migrants stuck in the camp outside Calais say politicians know nothing about them nor the desperate conditions they are living in'. *The Guardian*, 30 July. Accessed 30 November 2016 at: www.theguardian.com/uk-news/2015/jul/30/calais-crisis-its-easier-to-leave-us-living-like-this-if-you-say-we-are-bad-people.

The Telegraph (2002) 'Sangatte refugee camp closes early', 11 May. Accessed 30 November 2016 at: www.telegraph.co.uk/news/1412258/Sangatte-refugee-camp-closes-early.html.

Varada Raj, K. (2006) 'Paradoxes on the borders of Europe'. *International Feminist Journal of Politics*, 8(4), pp. 512–534.

Wall, S. (2012) 'Britain and Europe'. *The Political Quarterly*, 83(2), pp. 1191–1203.

4   The visualizing of Calais

Introduction

Calais has been a space of fluctuating media interest and shifting visualities since the emergence of the Jungle in 2003. Earlier media coverage of the jungle accompanied fewer visual depictions of their living conditions or daily existence beyond the threat they posed to their immediate environment. However, changing visuality from 2014 was marked by a surge in the number of images and in a diversification of imaging techniques that visually linked past and present events in Calais with the Mediterranean. There was also a shift in the focus of attention whether it be living conditions, daily life and community or by 2016 preparation for and the final apocalyptic destruction of Jungle 2. The refugee as an object of suffering and trauma is the subject of an abject gaze where the corporeal body is both a non-entity and invisible. Both death and the accident are ascribed to it, as inhabitants in this 'state of exception'. We examine these aesthetics of trauma and violence in the liminal space of Calais through its manifest visuality.

In September 2009 in the full glare of media cameras, riot police demolished an informal refugee camp near the port of Calais known as 'the Jungle' (Ibrahim, 2011; Howarth and Ibrahim, 2012; Ibrahim and Howarth, 2015a). The French government legitimized their overt actions, claiming that the Jungle had become a base for people traffickers who were targeting the UK as their ultimate destination. The militant action was welcomed by the British newspapers as constituting decisive action by the French to counter illegal migration across the Channel. The demolition of the Jungle became a major news event for British media where the spectacle of police brutality provided a theatre of cruelty with images of riot police and mighty bulldozers juxtaposed against flattened tents and tearful migrants. The demolition event of 2009 was devised as a media spectacle by the authorities to impress their spatial control over Calais. As such, the images centralized the demolition machine, with the refugees being a minute side act. The dominant images of 2016 centralized the apocalyptic in violent protests by refugees and anarchists, the mass 'exodus' of the camp inhabitants through forced evictions, the fires that engulfed the camp and the heavy machinery sent in to erase what had not been consumed by the flames. Our analysis of Calais reveals a shifting visuality from 2004 to 2016, where the pleasure in the media rituals of demolition is first replaced by an intrusive, inquisitive and transgressive gaze into the Other and then with a macabre fascination with the blaze that engulfs the camp and its erasure by heavy machinery, reducing a bustling camp to a lunar wasteland.

Not only did the events shift, so did the invitation to gaze. While the 2009 destruction was a spectacle, the five camp demolitions in 2014 and 2015 were relatively low-key events with only a handful of journalists present and relatively few images capturing the destruction. The discourse justifying destruction had shifted from rooting out lawlessness to dealing with public health concerns (Allen, 2015). Journalists re-engaged with the three demolitions in 2016, rendering them global spectacles, the events surrounding and entailing their destruction made visible through video-clips and slideshows of protests, evacuation and fire.

Despite the stark imagery of the first demolition, new camps sprung up overnight to replace those destroyed. The French police then continued their ritual of razing these down to the ground with their mammoth bulldozers. Hence the jungles of 2009 never really disappeared and even after what was planned as the final denouement in October 2016, new 'secret' camps sprung up in the valleys and smaller towns or villages around Calais. The camps remained liminal spaces of what Agamben terms the 'state of exception' inhabited by 'bare life'; a form of life whose status is indistinct and not governed by conventional law or politics.

The Calais refugee and the demolition of the camps courted media attention in 2009 and the number of stories on the crisis gained prominence again from April 2014 (see Table 4.1). The Calais crisis came back into media scrutiny due to bigger events in the Mediterranean, where unprecedented numbers of refugees were risking their lives in overcrowded and rickety boats. From 2013 the death toll from shipwrecks in the Mediterranean rose as refugees fled conflict and persecution in North Africa, but in April 2015 a smuggler's boat carrying 950 people, some locked in the hold, capsized off Libya's coast leaving only 28 survivors in what is believed to be the Mediterranean's deadliest known migrant tragedy.

Coverage of Calais also surged (see Table 4.1) during the summer of discontent in 2015 when French ferry workers went on strike and blocked freight access to the port between June and September, causing major disruptions to truckers and holidaymakers. There was an unprecedented proliferation of coverage of the 'Calais crisis', but it also tended to fold in the wider migrations happening across the Mediterranean with refugees fleeing from Somalia, Eritrea and Syria.

In Calais, the increased reporting and visuality into the camps was accompanied by an attendant curiosity with what was creating agony for the holidaymakers, port workers and truckers. The tragic image of Alan Kurdi on 2 September 2015, dead on the beach, ignited further interest in the Calais crisis, which saw a surge in photo coverage of both the Mediterranean and Calais crisis. This death event conflicted with the media spectacle where the public pity emerged through the exemplary of the dead child washed ashore. There was also a renewed awareness and interest in the plight of the lone or 'unaccompanied' children in the camp. It led to increased curiosity about the crisis with the phenomenon of 'voluntourism' where volunteers started to converge on Calais both through curiosity and an emerging politics of pity (see Ibrahim, 2010).

Gaze and the Calais refugee

The camp is a political site where law and order is suspended yet amenable to extreme forces of the sovereign state. For Agamben (1998, 2000), the camp rather than the city becomes a biopolitical space of exception where the West in its sociological imagination of being under siege post-9/11 has increasingly implemented harsher immigration and asylum policies despite the legal instruments of human rights and their idealized normative of a democratic entity. Agamben invokes the need to review the notion of the spatial politics of power, particularly the spatial logic of the camp in terms of inclusion and exclusion, belonging and dispossession. The Calais camps inhabiting an exceptional, marginal and peripheral space were rendered invisible and nonvisible as illegal entities. Labelled as a 'migrant camp' they are stripped of every political status and reduced completely to naked life (Agamben, 1998; 2000; Figure 4.1). According to Agamben, camps are paradoxically both outside the normal juridical order and yet somehow internal to that order. As such, people in the camps 'move about in a zone of indistinction between the outside and the inside, the exception and the rule, the licit and the illicit' (1998, p. 40). He argues that in such a permanent spatial arrangement the refugees become produced as bare life by sovereign powers. The 'bare life' becomes the reference in distinguishing the 'politically qualified' subject and equally in shoring up the borders of a sovereign political community.

Agamben's *homo sacer* or 'bare life' envisaged the expendable and wounded as both the target of sovereign violence and state of exception. For Agamben bare life is 'a zone of indistinction and continuous transition between man and beast' (1998, p. 109). As such, the inclusion in the polis

Figure 4.1 Bird's-eye view of the Calais Jungle
Source: Malachy Browne. January 2016. © BY-SA 2.0 Generic licence.

is precisely through its exclusion and through unlimited violation that is not deemed illegal. Hence, Western biopolitics is defined through the sovereign power and bare life. *Homo sacer* as a figure stands outside human and divine law while being the object of sovereign violence, which exceeds the force of law and yet is authorized by the law. The banished figure of the *homo sacer* can be killed with impunity yet not deemed sacred for religious sacrifice or a political subject to be accorded juridical law. For Agamben, as modern politics becomes a quest for new racialized and gendered targets in the politics of exclusion, they create a category of the 'living dead' (1998, p. 130). The refugee, the migrant or the inmates of Guantanamo Bay become the manifest species of bare life, reflecting the new forms of domination and the hidden ground within Western democracies; here the borders can ignite these regimes of control through policies of exclusion, a suspension of law, a state of exception, or at times an indistinction between norm and exception.

The inhabitants of the camps were constructed through a border politics as illegal corporal bodies presenting material risks to the ordered spaces of White suburbia and as economic opportunists seeking to storm into Britain to exploit their liberal benefit system. They posed the risk of denigrating the environment with their uncouth and criminal activities. These dehumanized narratives made their deaths and accidents crossing the border not deserving of pity or empathy (see Ibrahim, 2011; Ibrahim and Howarth, 2015b; Ibrahim and Howarth, 2015c). The images that accompanied the first jungle invited public gaze through these readings of inserting order over the bodies that contaminated a porous fortress Europe. The surge in images in 2014 and the subsequent trauma of Alan Kurdi's death image on the beach produced a counter-visuality that was as conflicted as the futility of the refugee predicament in Calais.

If Alan Kurdi's images produced a disruption to the refugee crisis, it also coalesced with a moment in press reporting to look beyond the cursory bodies damaged or demised through their passage across the borders. The new visuality surging through the proliferation of media images from 2014, fragmented reporting on the issue where it was no longer possible to ignore the disaster events of boats capsizing in the Mediterranean, particularly with Germany viewing the events as a humanitarian crisis despite the UK government's reluctance to be drawn into it. Visual connections were made by inserting images, video clips and slideshows of the 2015 port workers strike into stories in 2016 of refugee protests against the demolition of the camp. Or slideshows depicting events in the Mediterranean or clashes on the Hungarian border into articles on Calais. A visual–narrative arc was thereby created that served to locate the latest developments in Calais within earlier ones and into a wider European crisis. What had been a comparatively small-scale and parochial Anglo-French border 'problem' was reconstituted through visual techniques as a microcosm of a bigger crisis, but the inability to manage it invited comparison with what Turkey, Greece and Germany were doing.

The increased gaze into the camps and its inhabitants since 2014 mark a moment of conflicted visuality where the refugee bodies are objects of interest and curiosity. Their personal spaces, bodily needs, and sanitation become objects of gaze that emerge through a discourse of cataloguing and documenting their depraved conditions, and in the process this gaze is just as disconcerting as the mammoth machine bulldozing their makeshift tents. It produces a gaze into the private realms without producing an intimacy to the Other. The distancing from the Other took another twist in 2016. Protests failed to prevent demolition and in a ritualistic humiliation of the subjugated, the inhabitants of the camp were forced to queue for spaces on buses, their meagre belongings packed into suitcases freely distributed by the authorities, and then dispersed to 'reception' centres around France.

The context of irregular migration into Europe

Compared to the preceding years, in 2014 the world was facing its biggest refugee and migration crisis since the Second World War (UNHCR, 2015a).

Millions of people, half of whom were children, have been uprooted due to conflict or persecution and stranded on the edges of society as the long-term internally displaced or as refugees. The degree of displacement as evident in the numbers of people forced out of their countries has required more coordination between states than before (UNHCR, 2015b). The scale of irregular migration into the EU surged in 2011 with the onset of the Arab Spring in Tunisia and continued when sub-Saharan African refugees to Libya began to flee post-Qaddafi unrest in 2010–2011 (Park, 2015). One major force of displacement has been the Syrian conflict, with further displacements in crisis zones, particularly Afghanistan, Somalia and Eritrea.

The EU has become a key destination for many from North Africa and the Middle East; however, the increased militarization of the Mediterranean and the Calais borders has made it the 'most dangerous destination' for irregular migration in the world due to mortality rates (IOM, 2014). According to the International Organization for Migration's (IOM) estimates more than 1 million migrants have reached Europe in 2015, many of whom did so by crossing the Mediterranean and some 3,692 migrants died in their attempts to reach Europe, outstripping the number of deaths in 2014 by more than 400 (IOM, 2014). Though the EU is facing one of its biggest ever challenges, its response has been fragmented and ad hoc, with some governments welcoming Syrian refugees but not those from Eritrea, Somalia and Afghanistan. The British government has prioritized the securing of borders rather than the protection of the rights of migrants and refugees.

The privileging of security in policy responses is a retreat from discourses of according protection and rights to refugees that emerged after the Second World War in international agreements on how civilians should be treated in war; particularly the right to seek sanctuary, claim asylum, and avoid penalties for illegal entry in search of these. These dominant discourses in Europe have been eroded in responses to a series of major developments starting with the break-up of the former Soviet Union, the Eastern bloc and Yugoslavia in the 1990s and more recently the turmoil in the Middle East and North Africa.

In Calais, a Red Cross shelter that had sought to provide sanctuary to refugees from the Balkans was closed in 2002. The shelter was seen as a magnet for migrants seeking to enter the UK. By labelling them as migrants, both the UK and French governments sought to avoid arrangements for refugees warranted under international agreements. The then Interior Minister Nicolas Sarkozy placed a de facto ban on semi or permanent shelters that continued when he became President. By creating a spectacle of the demolition of the informal camps, they hoped to present it as a deterrent to more camps sprouting up in 2009. The François Hollande government elected in 2012 in contrast came under increased pressure from local politicians, humanitarian organizations and the UN, which in 2015 labelled the living conditions of the refugees as an 'indictment on society' (Taylor, 2015). Hollande's government equally had to respond to emergency measures to bring the informal camps up to minimum international standards in terms of running water, sanitation and lighting.

Beyond the stance of the UK and French governments to the scale of migration from conflict zones, the reaction of the newspapers to what they deemed and reported as a migrant problem is pertinent to the contextualization of imaging Calais. The newspapers in the UK mirrored the government's assertions that the issue should be cast through the lens of illegal immigration. As such, the negative depictions of the jungle need to be located within the resumption of a decade-long 'media campaign' against immigration policies (Parliament, 2007a). Most of Britain's national newspapers are ideologically conservative, however anti-immigration policy discourses are discernible across the broad political spectrum of British national newspapers (Ibrahim and Howarth, 2015c). Even before emergence of the Jungle, a dominant theme across all the newspapers was of immigration policy failure and the need to address this urgently. The most critical, though, were the mid-market titles such as the *Express* and *Daily Mail* which framed this failure in terms of government abdication of moral responsibility to protect Britons and migrants from exploitation by criminal networks.

Analysis of the images in the newspaper coverage

During the first phase between 2004 and 2009, the first photographs that were used (see Table 4.1) tended to focus mainly on flimsy shelters but from 2008 there was growing focus on squalor. The occasional map drew attention to the geographical proximity of the camp to Britain and aerial images created the sense of a settlement sprawling out of control. Together these visually legitimized demolition in September 2009. The French authorities

Table 4.1 Articles and images of the migrant jungles of Calais

	2004	2005	2006	2007	2008	2009	2010	2011	2012	2013	2014	2015	2016	TOTAL
# of articles on 'Calais AND Jungle'*	6	0	2	7	27	131	16	7	4	5	39	388	723	1334
# of images in articles on 'Calais AND Jungle'*	7	0	0	3	31	209	127	4	4	33	235	5195	9399	15247

invited the media, effectively turning the brutal destruction into a visual spectacle in which images proliferated. The period after demolition was marked by the emergence of new smaller jungles and a lull in reporting on Calais from 2011 till the end of 2013.[1]

There was renewed media interest in 2014 and 2015, manifest in an increase in articles and a surge in the imaging of the jungles of Calais (see Table 4.1, Figure 4.2). The second phase in the visual turn in Calais was contextualized within accounts of shipwrecks and deaths in the Mediterranean which drew attention to the unfolding humanitarian crisis in North Africa. As the number of inhabitants of the new jungle grew, coverage of Calais began to climb again, and it spiked in July 2015 when the French ferry workers strike brought a new visibility and visuality to the camps. Imaging techniques also diversified during this period creating a temporal–spatial intertextuality that linked past and present, the distant and the proximate. Aerial images that in 2009 had accompanied demolition stories, were recycled into visual comparisons of the size of Jungle 1 and Jungle 2 (Akbar, 2015) as if to reassert the futility of government attempts to control 'illegal' migration. Spatial intertextualities were constructed through maps that tracked the movement of refugees from their homeland to Calais (see Fjellberg, 2015) and Britain (Paton, 2015) and marked the spaces where

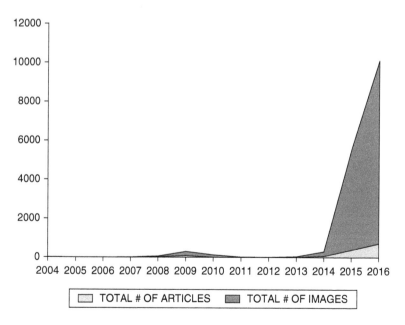

Figure 4.2 The visual turn: imaging the Jungles of Calais, 2004–2016

new security fences were erected. They were also constructed through the embedding of slideshows of events in the Mediterranean or on the Hungarian border into stories of Calais refugees. Such spatial-temporal intertextualities served to create a visual narrative that contextualized events within the genealogy of the jungles of Calais and reconstituted a relatively small-scale and 'parochial' Anglo-French border problem (Goldhammer, 2016) as a microcosm of a bigger geopolitical crisis engulfing Europe.

Juxtaposed against this visual geopolitics was a moment of conflicted visuality where the refugee bodies became objects of interest and curiosity. In the second half of 2015, attention shifted to a voyeuristic fascination as imaging techniques diversified further with photo essays with 'life in the camp' (Cox, 2015; Smith, Lane and Fidler, 2015). The images captured a pseudo-normality of social and domestic activity by day and desperate attempts to cross the channel at night. The social centred on the creation of the community spaces and self-organizing initiatives of the inhabitants motivated by the desire for the 'camp to be a place to live and not just survive' (Halliday and Graham-Harrison, 2015). The domestic privileged the personal spaces, bodily needs, and sanitation of the inhabitants of the camp who became objects of gaze that emerged through a discourse of cataloguing and documenting their depraved conditions, and in the process this gaze is just as disconcerting as the mammoth machine bulldozing their makeshift tents. It produces a gaze into the private realms without producing an intimacy to the Other.

The third phase of the visual turn emerged during 2016. Media attention and imaging continued to surge, and the techniques adopted in the earlier phase proliferated but the visual focus shifted to the 'progressive dismantling' of the camp in three stages, culminating in its final erasure in October of that year. Most of the key events were thematically organized into slide shows or embedded in news stories that created the sense that the refugee camps were at 'crisis point' and these included violent protests against demolition and that were linked visually to protests elsewhere in Europe, the 'mass exodus' (Bulman, 2016; Sheldrick, 2016; Figueiredo, 2016) as a result of the forced eviction or evacuation from the camp and the final images of the conflagration that engulfed the camp and the final erasure of what remained with heavy machinery including bulldozers and diggers.

Spectacle of demolition, violence, and brutality

The depictions of violence in Calais are both embodied and spatially arranged through the politics of the border. Violence appropriates a duality; there is violence inflicted on refugees' bodies by their restriction of movement and the frustration that arises from that and there is the violence of the sovereign state in the liminal state of exception in Calais. This dual-ity means that the displaced exercise power over their own bodies through the risk they take to cross the border. Equally, the sovereign power wields bio-political power on these contaminants who weaken the security of their borders. The third aspect of violence is the camp itself, where the inhabitants pose further danger to themselves (i.e. women and children), demarcating the camp through its inherent atavism as a space of 'madness and despair' (Pugliese, 2002). The fourth aspect of the violence is the violence inflicted by refugees or migrants on others through the adoption of 'more aggressive tactics' for instance setting strategically placed obstacles in the road alight and hurling stones, metal spears and logs at the cabin in a bid to bring the lorry to a halt so they can board (Batchelor, 2015; Campbell, 2016).

The interior gaze into the camp marks its instability within a wider con-text of violence unleashed on its inhabitants. Joseph Pugliese (2002, p. 1) argues that the spacio-temporal logic of the camp induces

> refugees to fall back on the one resource left to them in the midst of the violence of indefinite incarceration: their bodies. Even as the body is bounded and imprisoned, it can exercise a power that will elude the mechanisms of repression and the desire for absolute control.

The readings of violence accrue dialectically both in the refugees' appropri-ation of the only resource left to them (i.e. their corporeal body) and equally the sovereign powers' quest to control these expendable entities. The imag-ing of the jungle as such unleashes an aesthetics of violence, captured in the refugees' interaction with the wider world and the authorities' initial attempts to outlaw the jungle and in their subsequent attempts to contain them within the demarcated spheres.

The imaging of Jungle 1 was dominated by the spectacle of the destruc-tion in September 2009 with coverage in most national dailies. These images centralized the machinery and its might in the destruction of the victim. The victims were diminished both in the lack of human focus on them and equally through their displacement. Their suffering was not the centric in these images. These demolitions stylized for the observer as a media event sought to impress readers that the French were enacting spa-tial control over their territory and to overcome criticism that there was inertia in dealing with the refugees. The military-style demolition organ-ized as a 'dawn raid' by riot police and flamethrowers, accompanied by bulldozers and chainsaws and in the full glare of the media was designed to quell public disquiet and to court the media gaze. A significant proportion of the British press welcomed the destruction of the camp as a sign that the French authorities were getting tough on the traffickers. The brutality as depicted through the images of tearful migrants remained as a prop in these imageries. These publicity stunts did not augur well with the French public and were perceived as futile in rooting out people traffickers (Hall, 2009). The five camp demolitions in 2014 and 2015 repeat similar scenes of bulldozers and cranes with refugees watching helplessly as their shelters are destroyed and police restraining them from going back to salvage their belongings. These were on a smaller scale compared to 2009 and by November 2015 had become a non-event for most journalists.

The visual turn during the 2015 summer of discontent captured more graphically than before the brutality of militarization, migrant-police engagements and the desperation of refugees leaping or sneaking aboard passing vehicles. Depictions of black smoke billowing from tyres set on fire by striking port workers combined with images of police cordons at the perimeter fence to the Channel Tunnel and black-clad riot police armed with shields, batons and tear gas straddling railway lines and roads showcase the extent of their vigilante gaze and the depictions of the 'troubles, risks and inconveniences' presented by the refugees to the public and authorities.

Beyond media representations, the imaging of Calais was expanded through user-generated content (UGC) captured through volunteers as well as those who encountered the scenes between the police and refugees in Calais. An inquiry was launched by a police watchdog after a video posted online by activist group Calais Migrant Solidarity (CMS) appeared to show officers stopping migrants on the road then shoving, kicking and beating them, pushing them over the guardrail and forcing them to the ground or spraying teargas at close range at refugees walking along the road (Samuel, 2015; Chrisafis, 2015). Another clip posted online showed a Hungarian lorry driver deliberately swerving in front of the refugees in the Calais 'war zone' and the inhabitants then scattering out of the way (Withnall, 2015). Such encounters became a game of violence enacted on the refugees. These images of cruelty and brutality against the refugees expanded the theatre of violence. The mainstream media in exhibiting UGC on their websites provided a counter-visuality to the migrant crisis in Calais. The UGC in some parts also re-inscribed the discourses of risk and paranoia evident from the 2009 reports of refugees invading white suburbia. A number of images showcased refugees breaking into the back of lorries travelling to Britain with captions stating that 'hooded men were running amok' and a 'baying mob brought a motorway to a standstill' as Calais was described as facing an invasion and descent into 'anarchy' (Gye, 2015; Sheldrick, 2015).

The desperation of the migrants during the summer of 2015 to enter the UK through the stalled vehicles in Calais was also captured in UGC, taken from a holiday coach of 'tourist terror' as migrants 'swarmed' around trucks and 'smashed their way' into the back of them (Newton, 2015). The 'native encounters with the jungle inhabitants' as such produced new forms of exhibits and imaginaries of the 'migrant'. These native encounters coalesced with images in media reports showing refugees walking or running alongside railway tracks littered with accounts of a teenager electrocuted climbing through holes in the old fencing or dangling a small child over it. There were also images of migrants clinging to the top of trucks or hanging onto the undercarriage, squeezing into tight spaces behind the cab or sneaking into the back then being forcibly removed by the police if spotted. Risk, death and injury became images of normality, and violence was inscribed as a corporeal reality as refugees sought to break free of their predicament.

The tragic consequences of such desperate measures were poignantly captured in images of a makeshift cemetery where wooden crosses mark the spots where 28 refugees have been buried in Calais, and one headstone marks the grave of baby Samir Khedija whose Eritrean mother had a miscarriage during an attempt to travel from Calais to England (Akbar, 2015). With women and children not immune to police violence, an up-close image captured a large bruise on the upper arm of a 16-year old girl which she alleges as the product of a police baton (Thornhill, 2014). Images also capture women and young girls scrambling through fences in a bid to board a freight train. There are also images of a young man pulling a young child over a barbed wire fence before helping her drop to the ground close to the high-speed tracks, those of children walking along the side of the road or the railway tracks and of a 10-year-old Eritrean boy squeezed into a gap in a cab by his 17-year old brother who vowed to get him to Britain before making the journey himself (Kelly, 2015). Children as the most precious commodity of the refugee become part of this violent imagery to redeem some form of legal status.

The chaotic and violent destruction of Jungle 2 in October 2016 was at odds not only with the 2009 demolition but also with the euphemistic official discourse of 'progressive dismantling'. In the weeks leading up to demolition, the refugees and migrants resisted evacuation and their protests turned violent with police resorting to water cannon, rubber bullets and tear gas canisters and the protestors responding by throwing stones through air hazy with smoke. Ultimately for many, resistance was futile and faced with forcible eviction thousands fled the camp. Many of those who remained queued peaceably for buses to disperse them to over 100 reception centres around France, but others were angry. A dismantlement that began calmly degenerated within three days of the operation into the 'apocalyptic' as some of the inhabitants in a final act of resistance set fire to their homes before the police could destroy them (McCrum, 2016) and in the ensuing chaos aid workers rushed to remove gas canisters before they exploded (Walker *et al.*, 2016). The situation was further worsened by official under-estimating of the number of children in the camp. Official plans had called for unaccompanied children to remain in Calais while their family reunification plans were considered, but processing stopped when the 1500 person container shelters were filled, and dozens of teenagers were abandoned, left to sleep in the jungle or on the streets 'exposed to violence, noise and fires that burned through the night'. Those that were placed in the container shelters were left unsupervised, sleeping in bare containers and left to roam around heavy machinery being used to dismantle and remove the remnants of the camp (Drogoul and Hanryon, 2016; England, 2016).

When the flames had subsided, heavy machinery flattened what fire had not destroyed, reducing a 'vast shantytown' housing up to 10,000 people to a 'barren wasteland' (Robinson, 2016). Not only had the shacks, tents and caravans disappeared, so too were the community spaces and the communities that used them broken up as inhabitants were dispersed around France. All that was left was a bleak emptiness of uninhabited scrubland against a backdrop of security fences reinforced with razor wire and surveillance cameras and the sterile white containers. Volunteers who had worked there for some time and seen the community grow described the emptiness as a 'surreal . . . eeriness', the camp songs and chatter in the library and school that had characterized a 'vibrant' community a 'distance memory' (Robinson, 2016). A slideshow depicting before and after showed in graphic detail the scale of what had been lost and the destruction (Elvey, 2016).

The wounded, dead and traumatized refugee imageries were juxtaposed with those of police brutality and authorities being in control of the situation. Doctors working with refugees reported growing numbers of migrants with trauma injuries including broken bones and cuts from police violence and from falling off trucks. Images in the media corroborated some of these claims, capturing ongoing 'skirmishes' with migrants challenging the cordons, running from the police or fleeing the spray from small canisters of tear gas fired by officers (Robinson *et al.*, 2015). But the witnessing by the doctors remained separate from the media tracts where, for example, charities and NGOs were utilizing new media platforms to highlight the plights of the refugees (see Ibrahim and Howarth, 2015a).

The spectacle of violence that engulfs the refugee's body makes it exemplary and an instrumental weapon in warning other prospective asylum seekers not to repeat this passage (Pugliese, 2002). The theatre of violence is part of the border politics of Calais, where the spatial politics inscribe the refugee bodies with violence, highlighting their expendability and equally the denigration of a humanitarian crisis into a 'deviant migrant' discourse of opportunism, hence absolving the state of its moral or legal obligations.

The physical site of the camp

Jungle 2 grew partly out of the humanitarian crisis in North Africa which had been building since 2011 and had turned the Mediterranean into an 'apocalyptic charnel house' and partly from the forcible movement in 2015 of the inhabitants of informal camps close to the port to a 'toleration' zone outside town where food and some showers were available (Han, 2015; O'Doherty, 2015). As the numbers in the camp grew, the sense of semi-permanence evolved incrementally as different communities self-organized. Somali shacks clustered around a large dining tent where they ate in groups (Cox, 2015; Wainwright, 2016); Sundanese also clustered around communal eating spaces with separate spaces for cooking together; Afghans lived more separately but set up restaurants along an emerging 'strip' for social gathering. The Eritrean community set up a nightclub in a dome-shaped structure which served as a theatre and gallery during the day. Images also showed an evolution in the construction of shelters from flimsy, rudimentary and ad hoc in Jungle 1 to also to variety of tents, caravans, containers.

As the numbers in the camp grew, there were a 'lot of beautiful initiatives' as refugee communities and volunteers became the 'architects' of a post-apocalyptic sociality of 'vibrant' community spaces, what Irish architect Grainne Hassett called a 'prototype city in the making' (Wainwright, 2016). By August 2016 there were 70 shops, cafés and restaurants as well as schools, a library, mosques and churches built by refugees, migrants and volunteers motivated by the desire for the 'camp to be a place to live and not just survive' (Halliday and Graham-Harrison, 2015; Figure 4.3). The resolve to do more than survive meant that, while the living conditions were justifiably damned as sub-standard for international refugee camps, Jungle 2 had a 'kind of life there that the UNHCR camps simply don't have . . . [and] the stages for strong social and cultural structures had somehow been forced out of nothing' (Wainwright, 2016). Another visitor to the camp saw in this proliferation of community spaces a culturally informed 'kind of urbanism, which felt very authentic, very deeply rooted in their culture[s]' most clearly manifest in how refugee communities organized their shelters (Wainwright, 2016). The final dismantling of the jungle did more than destroy shelters, it destroyed the community spaces of respite and, in dispersing the inhabitants, the self-organizing capabilities in the camp.

Figure 4.3 St Michael's Church in the Calais Jungle seen from the south side
Source: By Liam Stoopdice. 17 January 2016. © BY-SA 4.0 International licence.

These endeavours to create spaces of semi-permanence and community were a resistance against mounting squalor, degradation and dehumanization. The endeavours were given added impetus by a French court order that gave authorities eight days to implement emergency measures to bring living conditions up to minimum international standards for refugee camps with the government allocating €18 million (£12.7 million) to do so (Holehouse, 2015). Thus, there is an increasing emphasis on images that install the semi-permanence of the camps through the provision of basic amenities. Making the camp a quasi-settlement infuses a 'spacio-temporal logic where the figure of the homo sacer is confined and bounded by the spatial-materiality of the camp, strictly delimiting the refugees' freedom of movement and marking the material borders of their existence. Due to the indefinite nature of the detention, the refugee is sentenced to a temporal open-endedness that knows no limits' (Pugliese, 2002). As such, Pugliese argues that the 'incarcerated refugee is forced to experience the vertiginous violence of "imprisonment-in-infinitude" which becomes the locus of the madness and the despair generating the uprisings and revolts in the detention centres'.

The consolidation of Jungle 2 as a quasi-settlement was depicted through aerial images showing it trebling in size into a mini-metropolis. The aerial views became cartographic impressions of its growth and, in many ways, confirmed the fears of the French and UK authorities that the jungle was sprawling out of control and infiltrating their ordered spaces. The images in 2014 and 2015 captured these transitions, such as refugees clustered around a mobile-charging site using multi-socket adaptors powered by a generator. The savage of Jungle 1 who was constantly robbed of his belongings and shelter was resurrected in these images with the ability to charge telecommunication equipment.

However, perhaps the most graphic divergence from Jungle 1 was the beginning of a sanitation system, not in the form of permanent waste water piping but in the provision of 50 chemical, porta-cabin toilets commonly used on building sites (Kelly, 2015). Earlier narratives and images of the camp portrayed it in squalor, filth, excrement and stench. As such, the images of porta-cabins and flushing toilets seem to suggest lifting the savage from his defecation-filled existence into redemption through the provision of basic amenities that he was not entitled to earlier. After a sustained criticism from UNHCR about the lack of standards in the camp, the French authorities announced they would make the 'New Jungle' a 'permanent fixture by providing running water and electricity to the site' (Bulman, 2016; Hall and Sparks, 2015). However, heavy rainfall in 2016 turned the camp into a swamp and the portable toilets were surrounded by water and mud, and virtually inaccessible. Nevertheless, despite its redemption through sanitation, the camp was forever saturated and associated with filth through images of litter, uncollected refuse, old boxes of food, surrounded by rats and infused with the smell of human waste.

The camp was no longer gendered through male presence. In 2014 and 2015, the first semi-formal shelters for women and children began to open in response to the increasing numbers of 'lone women queuing up' to get into Britain and 'desperate mothers dragging their babies 5000 miles' to Calais (Ellicott, 2014). On the instigation of Natacha Bouchart, the Mayor of Calais, new 'Sangatte-style' sheltered accommodation was opened for them and after a court order in October 2015, authorities began for the first time to identify children arriving in the camp. Although some women and children stayed in the shelters, these filled up within weeks and the rest were forced to live in the Jungle 2 camp. The Jungle as a space of insistent and sustained violence is communicated through the fears and anxieties of women and children incarcerated there. The media reports revealed that women had admitted to sleeping six to a tent for security reasons as they lived in constant fear of being raped after dark when men would drink and fight. Mothers with their children reportedly hid in tents during the day or inside a locked detention centre to avoid being assaulted by the men around them. Others had reportedly been forced into prostitution by pimps as a way of protecting themselves against gangs and one charity claimed it locked the gates at night to protect the women and children in its shelter.

The intrusive gaze into the private realms of the refugee created an aesthetic of violence as well as an acknowledgement of the refugee body as a non-sacred entity, as the notions of 'private' and 'public' become blurred in the camp through the transgressive media gaze and public consumption of the camp. The imagining of Jungle 1 had included snapshots of daily life in the camp, but these were mainly outside scenes with a glimpse from a distance into a mosque with Muslims praying before the raid and the occasional photograph taken inside a tent of bedding and clothes or of baking bread. In contrast, media attention on Jungle 2, at least from August 2015, expanded to include the visualization of life inside the jungle. Some created the appearance of 'normality among the harsh conditions' (Smith, 2015) including migrants relaxing with 'universal' pleasures such as playing football or dominoes and women and children talking in groups outside the church, a typical scene in many parts of the world where Christians gather on Sundays, or children playing pool in the Kids Café (Figure 4.4).

Despite reports and images that sought to look inside the camps, these constituted a form of constructed aesthetics to visualize the Other. While it disrupted the earlier hostile reports of Jungle 1, the more intrusive gaze of Jungle 2 reignited the dispossessed nature of the camp and its inhabitants, where their lives and predicaments were public but the resolution a private matter for them to confront and encounter through the risks they took with their own bodies or those they inflicted on their most sacred possessions (i.e. their offspring), reiterating Pugliese's (2002) prophecy of the camp as a space of madness and despair.

The visual turn in imaging the refugee crisis in Calais beginning in 2013 and building momentum from 2014 needs to be contextualized against earlier media representations of Jungle 1. The increased and interiorized gaze of Jungle 2 offers a counter-visuality to earlier depictions of the refugee settlements. This counter-visuality, while not completely dichotomized from the communal politics of pity, produces the camp as an unresolved site of human struggle. The gaze afforded through the media enables both material and symbolic readings of the camp in analysing the images. As a site of unresolved human trauma, the visuality produces a sustained documentary of instability produced through war, strife and conflict across the world.

Figure 4.4 Kids Space – children's library in the Jungle refugee camp
Source: By Katja Ulbert, 02 January 2016. © BY-SA 4.0 International licence.

The camp freezes time and space, entrapping its inhabitants in a bubble of futility while their lives are on hold infinitely. The media gaze opens yet more probing ethical questions on the plight of the homo sacer, the by-product of sovereign power; constituted by it yet disowned through its politics of exclusion.

Note

1 We examined the articles of the Calais crisis from 2004 when the first mention of the 'Jungle' appeared in national newspapers (Coates, 2004). Our examination focused on the online versions of the four main tabloid newspapers: *The Sun, The Mirror, The Express* and *Daily Mail* as well as the five main qualities, i.e. *Financial Times, The Times, The Telegraph, The Guardian* and *The Independent*. The corpus also included the Sunday counterparts of tabloids and broadsheets, except for *The Sun*. We also supplemented this with a search on UK Online database. Our combined search on 'calais and jungle' on the database and the online archives between 2000 and 2016 generated 1344 articles and the use of 15,247 images (See Table 4.1).

References

Agamben, G. (1998) *Homo Sacer: Sovereign Power and Bare Life*. Stanford, CA: Stanford University Press.

Agamben, G. (2000) *Means Without End: Notes on Politics*. Minneapolis, MN: University of Minnesota Press.

Akbar, J. (2015) 'The price of getting to Britain: Makeshift cemetery in Calais holds the refugees who didn't make it . . . and the graveyard is only set to grow'. *Mail Online*, 01 November. Accessed 30 November at: www.dailymail.co.uk/news/article-3299151/The-price-getting-Britain-Makeshift-cemetery-Calais-holds-refugees-didn-t-make-graveyard-set-grow.html.

Allen, P. (2015) 'French to bulldoze camp where hundreds of immigrants are gathering to enter Britain illegally as a "risk to public health"'. *Mail Online*, 22 May. Accessed 30 November at: www.dailymail.co.uk/news/article-2636335/French-bulldoze-camp-hundreds-immigrants-are.html.

Batchelor, T. (2015) 'Calais crisis: Now migrants target UK-bound ferries as Eurotunnel security is stepped up'. *The Express*, 06 August. Accessed 11 January 2018 at: www.express.co.uk/news/world/596442/Calais-crisis-Eurotunnel-security-migrants-target-UK-ferries.

Bulman, M. (2016) 'French police accused of stealing from migrants to stop them leaving Jungle'. *The Independent*, 15 October. Accessed 11 January 2018 at: www.independent.co.uk/news/world/europe/french-police-calais-jungle-migrants-refugees-human-rights-brutality-a7362281.html.

Campbell, B. (2016) 'Flames licked at our wheels in the Calais war zone'. *The Sunday Times*, 04 September. Accessed 11 January 2018 at: www.thetimes.co.uk/article/flames-licked-at-our-wheels-in-the-calais-war-zone-md76ftkrd.

Chrisafis, A. (2015) 'French police watchdog investigates video of alleged abuse of Calais migrants'. *The Guardian*, 13 May. Accessed 30 November at: www.theguardian.com/world/2015/may/13/french-police-video-calais-migrants.

Coates, S. (2004) 'Desperate refugees hide in "jungle" outside Calais'. *The Times*, 24 August.

Cox, H. (2015) 'Life in the Calais migrant "jungle" with Sultan from Sudan'. *Financial Times*. 27 August. Accessed at: www.ft.com/cms/s/0/d46bc7ee-468b-11e5-af2f-4d6e0e5eda22.html#slide11.

Drogoul, F. and Hanryon, S. (2016) 'What next for refugees after demolition of the Calais camp'. *British Medical Journal*, 355 (November) pp. 1–2.

Ellicott, C. (2014) 'Now desperate mothers drag their BABIES 5,000 miles to squalid Calais refugee camps to find husbands who have already crossed channel into Britain'. *Daily Mail*, 04 August. Accessed 30 November at: www.dailymail.co.uk/news/article-2804580/Now-desperate-mothers-drag-BABIES-5-000-miles-squalid-Calais-refugee-camps-husbands-crossed-channel-Britain.html.

Elvey, S. (2016) 'Eerie Calais Jungle pictures show barely recognisable camp is now barren scrubland after bulldozers demolished it'. *Mirror*, 11 November. Accessed 18 January 2018 at: www.mirror.co.uk/news/uk-news/eerie-calais-jungle-pictures-show-9241237.

England, C. (2016) 'Refugee children sleeping rough on site of destroyed Calais Jungle – three days after camp was "cleared"'. *The Independent*, 29 October. Accessed 100 January 2018 at: www.independent.co.uk/news/world/europe/calais-jungle-latest-refugee-children-unaccompanied-minors-camp-migrants-destroyed-relocated-moved-a7386551.html.

Figueiredo, A. (2016) Home Office taken to HIGH COURT for failing to protect Calais migrant children. *Express Online*, 16 October. Accessed 11 January 2018 at: www.express.co.uk/news/uk/721769/Calais-migrant-children-failed-Home-Office-which-faces-COURT.

Fjellberg, A. (2015) 'The boys who could see England'. *The Sunday Times*. 02 August. Accessed at: www.thesundaytimes.co.uk/sto/newsreview/article1587976.ece.

Goldhammer, A. (2016) 'Burning down the Jungle of Calais'. *Foreign Policy*, 29 February. Accessed 11 January 2018 at: http://foreignpolicy.com/2016/02/29/burning-down-the-jungle-of-calais/.

Gye, H. (2015) Migrants are hitting the NHS before they even reach our shores – £2.5m of medicines are destroyed after lorries carrying them are breached in Calais'. *Mail Online*, 09 August. Accessed 30 November at: www.dailymail.co.uk/news/article-3191059/Medicines-destroyed-lorries-carrying-breached-Calais.html.

Hall, B. (2009) 'Refugee groups attack police clearance of Calais camp'. *Financial Times*, 23 September. Accessed 30 November at: www.ft.com/cms/s/0/ac3766b8-a7d9-11de-b0ee-00144feabdc0.html?siteedition=uk.

Hall, J. and Sparks, I. (2015) 'French MP blames Britain's "black jobs market" for Calais migrant problem as "New Jungle" camp home to 3,000 Africans gets permanent electricity and water supplies'. *Mail Online*, 22 June. Accessed 30 November at: www.dailymail.co.uk/news/article-3134285/Calais-New-Jungle-electricity-water-migrant-camp-permanent-Switzerland-.

Halliday, J. and Graham-Harrison, E. (2015) 'Calais migrants abandon plans for life in UK and start learning French: There's a mosque, shops and now a school. The students and volunteer teachers want the camp to be a place to live, not just survive'. *The Observer*, 03 August. Accessed 11 January 2018 at: www.theguardian.com/world/2015/aug/01/calais-camp-migrants-abandon-uk-learn-french.

Han, J. (2015) 'New Jungle in Calais'. *Financial Times*, 25 June. Accessed 11 January 2018 at: http://blogs.ft.com/photo-diary/2015/06/new-jungle-in-calais/.

Holehouse, M. (2015) 'Migrant crisis: European Council president Tusk warns Schengen on brink of collapse'. *The Telegraph*, 13 November. Accessed 30 November at: www.telegraph.co.uk/news/worldnews/europe/eu/11991098/Migrant-crisis-Donald-Tusk-warns-that-Schengen-is-on-brink-of-collapse-latest-news.html.

Howarth, A. and Ibrahim, Y. (2012) 'Threat and suffering: The liminal space of "the Jungle"', in H. Andrews and L. Roberts (eds) *Liminal Landscapes: Travel, Experience and Spaces In-between*. London: Routledge, pp. 200–216.

Ibrahim, Y. (2010) 'Distant suffering and postmodern subjectivity: The communal politics of pity'. *Nebula*, 7(1–2): 122–135.

Ibrahim, Y. (2011) 'Constructing the Jungle, distance framing in the *Daily Mail*'. *International Journal of Media and Cultural Politics*, 7, 315–331.

Ibrahim, Y. and Howarth, A. (2015a) 'Sounds of the Jungle: Re-humanizing the migrant'. *JOMEC*, June.

Ibrahim, Y. and Howarth, A. (2015b) 'Space and the Jungle in Calais: Space making through place, policy, human movement and media', in E. Thorsen, D.J.H. Savigny and J. Alexander (eds) *Media, Margins and Civic Agency*. Basingstoke: Palgrave-MacMillan.

Ibrahim, Y. and Howarth, A. (2015c) 'Space construction in media reporting: A study of the migrant space in the "Jungles" of Calais'. *Fast Capitalism*, 12. Accessed at: www.uta.edu/huma/agger/fastcapitalism/12_1/Ibrahim-Howarth-Space-Construction.htm.

International Organization for Migration. (2014) *Fatal Journeys: Tracking Lives Lost During Migration* [Online]. Accessed 30 November at: www.iom.int/statements/iom-releases-new-data-migrant-fatalities-worldwide-almost-40000-2000.

Kelly, T. (2015) 'Up you go! Brother hoists boy of just TEN onto Calais lorry bound for Britain as shock figures show number of stowaways to the UK has surged by 200 per cent in just a year'. *Daily Mail*, 26 June. Accessed 30 November: www.dailymail.co.uk/news/article-3139602/Up-Boy-just-10-helped-Calais-lorry-bound-Britain-number-stowaways-UK-surges-200.html.

McCrum, K. (2016) 'Chaotic Calais Jungle now a barren desert one month after authorities removed thousands of migrants'. *Mirror.co.uk*, 24 November. Accessed 11.01.2018 at: www.mirror.co.uk/news/world-news/chaotic-calais-jungle-now-barren-9324086.

Mirzoeff, N. (2011) 'The right to look'. *Critical Inquiry*, 37, 473–496.

Newton, J. (2015) 'Tourists' terror at Calais: Coach passengers capture shocking footage as migrants surround their vehicle and smash their way onto a lorry heading to the UK'. *Daily Mail*, 15 June. Accessed 30 November at: www.dailymail.co.uk/news/article-3124280/Tourists-terror-Calais-Coach-passengers-capture-shocking-footage-migrants-surround-vehicle-smash-way-lorry-heading-UK.html.

O'Doherty, I. (2015) 'Migrants in the Med: Why devil is in the details'. *Irish Independent*, 05 July. Accessed 11 January 2018 at: www.independent.ie/entertainment/television/odoherty-migrants-in-the-med-why-devil-is-in-the-detail-31347645.html.

Park, J. (2015) *Europe's Migration Crisis*. New York: Council of Foreign Relations.

Paton, G. (2015) 'British drivers run gauntlet of knife-wielding migrants'. *The Times*. 27 June. Accessed 11 January 2018 at: www.thetimes.co.uk/tto/news/politics/article4481521.ece.

Pugliese, J. (2002) 'Penal asylum: Refugees, ethics, hospitality'. *Borderlands*, 1–8. Accessed at: www.borderlands.net.au/vol1no1_2002/pugliese.html.

Robinson, J. (2016) 'What a difference a month makes: Before and after photos show how Calais "jungle" camp for 10,000 migrants is now a bulldozed wasteland'. *MailOnline*, 11 November. Accessed at: www.dailymail.co.uk/news/article-3927176/What-difference-month-makes-photos-Calais-jungle-camp-10-000-migrants-bulldozed-wasteland.html.

Robinson, M., Glanfield, E., Ellicott, C. and Wright, S. (2015) 'Fury after PM warns of "swarm": As police seize stowaway migrants across South, Cameron is attacked for "likening them to insects"'. *Mail Online*, 30 July. Accessed 30 November at: www.dailymail.co.uk/news/article-3180063/British-police-stop-lorry-M20-just-15-miles-Folkestone-arrest-12-migrants-patrols-stepped-sides-Channel-days-migrants-storming-tunnel.html.

Samuel, H. (2015) 'Police inquiry launched over film showing "police brutality" against UK-bound Calais migrants'. *The Telegraph*, May 12. Accessed 30 November at: www.telegraph.co.uk/news/worldnews/europe/france/11600461/Police-inquiry-launched-over-film-showing-police-brutality-against-UK-bound-Calais-migrants.html.

Sheldrick, G. (2015) 'The migrant invasion: Dramatic pictures show Calais crisis descend into anarchy'. *The Express*, 18 June. Accessed 30 November at: www.express.co.uk/news/world/585189/Calais-migrant-crisis-immigrantion-anarchy.

Sheldrick, G. (2016) 'REVEALED: Calais migrant chaos has cost UK taxpayers more than £90 MILLION over two years'. *Express Online*, 12 October. Accessed at: www.express.co.uk/news/uk/720230/Calais-migrants-chaos-cost-UK-taxpayers-90million-Amber-rudd-bernard-Bernard-Cazeneuve.

Smith, S. (2015) 'Migrant life in Calais Jungle refugee camp – a photo essay'. *The Guardian*, 05 October. Accessed 30 November at: www.theguardian.com/media/ng-interactive/2015/aug/10/migrant-life-in-calais-jungle-refugee-camp-a-photo-essay.

Smith, S., Lane, G. and Fidler, M. (2015) 'Migrant life in Calais Jungle refugee camp – a photo essay'. *The Guardian*. 10 August. Accessed 11 January 2018 at: www.theguardian.com/media/ng-interactive/2015/aug/10/migrant-life-in-calais-jungle-refugee-camp-a-photo-essay.

Taylor, M. (2015) 'UN migration representative: Calais camp is an indictment on society'. *The Guardian*, 23 September. Accessed 30 November at: www.theguardian.com/world/2015/sep/23/un-migration-calais-jungle-camp-peter-sutherland.

Thornhill, T. (2014) 'Calais under siege: Migrants march through streets demanding human rights protection amid warnings French port is being overwhelmed'. *Mail Online*, 08 October. Accessed on 30 November at: www.dailymail.co.uk/news/article-2744837/Alarming-footage-emerges-migrants-vaulting-16-foot-fence-ferries-Calais-amid-warnings-shutting-port-just-problem-elsewhere.html.

UNHCR (2015a) 'High-level UN event tackles biggest refugee and migration crisis since Second World War'. Accessed at: www.un.org/apps/news/story.asp?NewsID=52074#.VnwXy1kSzAE.

UNHCR (2015b) 'Worldwide displacement hits all-time high as war and persecution increase'. Accessed at: www.unhcr.org/558193896.html.

Wainwright, O. (2016) 'We built this city: How the refugees of Calais became its architects'. *The Guardian*, 08 June. Accessed at: www.theguardian.com/artanddesign/2016/jun/08/refugees-calais-jungle-camp-architecture-festival-barbican.

Walker, P., Weaver, M. and Pujol-Mazzini, A. (2016) Calais camp refugees burn shelters as demolitions resume. *The Guardian*, 01 March. Accessed 11 January 2018 at: www.theguardian.com/world/2016/mar/01/french-riot-police-teargas-jungle-calais-camp-evictions.

Withnall, A. (2015) 'Video shows Hungarian lorry driver deliberately swerving at refugees in Calais "war zone"'. *The Independent*, 03 November. Accessed 30 November at: www.independent.co.uk/news/world/europe/video-shows-hungarian-lorry-driver-deliberately-swerving-at-refugees-in-calais-war-zone-a6754461.html.

5 The 'lone child' in Calais

From invisibility to the Dubs Amendment[1]

Introduction

One of the most unsettling and seemingly unresolved figures in the Calais refugee crisis is the figure of the child. Particularly, that of the unaccompanied child. Often the treatment of children and their protection as a social and ethical imperative in society is a hallmark of a civilized society. Little in life arouses more indignation and demands more moral judgement than the suffering of children where their suffering can be symbolic of the exploitation of the powerless, the abuse of the defenceless and the defiling of the innocent (King, 1997, p. 1). Children even though they are considered as social actors are seen as problematic entities in society, they are not seen as fully rational beings; lacking in wisdom, needing protection, they are often presented as having needs which have to be met rather than their rights upheld rendering them as silent and invisible entities in adult society (King, 1997, pp. 474–476).

Europe's response to lone children became an issue of both moral scrutiny and ethical introspection in view of its trajectory of the Holocaust as a European genocide in contravention of its own imagination of superiority through its civilizing project of Enlightenment and its attendant morality. The treatment of the child refugee became an area of renewed scrutiny through the UK's nostalgic recall of its own role in the 'Kindertransport' where a series of rescue efforts brought thousands of refugee children out from Nazi-occupied Europe between 1938 and 1939. The British authorities had agreed to allow an unspecified number of children under the age of 17 to enter the country, spurred by public opinion and the efforts of refugee aid committees. The UK's seemingly open-door policy and congenial attitudes in rescuing the Jewish children would return to provide a contrast to the ethical standing of the UK in the Calais refugee crisis.

The invisible children in Calais

In the Jungles of Calais children remained hidden and conjoined to the general composition of displaced bodies without distinction. For a long period of time they did not emerge as distinct figures in media imagery despite concerns raised by the UN and aid agencies as early as 2008 (cf. Mougne, 2010). While the Jungles had been a feature of the Calais and Dunkirk landscape for nearly two decades, the figure of the child refugee only gained prominence and became politicized in 2015. Calais is symbolic of a bottleneck where the displaced are entrapped – unable to go back to their country of origin for fear of war or persecution but also impeded from moving on by ever tightening British immigration policies and increased securitization around the ferry port and Tunnel (and more recently along the access routes). This bottleneck of the trapped bodies would unleash a desperate ritual of refugees embarking on life-threatening attempts to stowaway on passing vehicles headed across the Channel. Children too became part of these rituals, posing extreme risk to their lives.

Categorized as 'dependents' in immigration rules and legislation, refugee children occupy a problematic space as legal entities. It has been recognized by the international and national communities that children are often overlooked as 'right bearers' and the need for specific instruments that afford them special consideration on the basis of their unique and vulnerable status (Bell, 2008, p. 9). This need for special attention towards the child and the voids in the recognition of their rights gained momentum, beginning with the UN Declaration of the Rights of the Child (1959) and subsequent enacted instruments between 1965 and 1996 that sought to awareness of the vulnerability of the child and strengthen protections and rights.[2]

A particularly vulnerable group in refugee crises are 'unaccompanied' children who are defined as 'separated from both parents and for whose care no person can be found who by law or custom has primary responsibility' (Ayotte and Williamson, 2000). Jacqueline Bhaba (2004, p. 141), in writing about separated children and forced migration, points out that 'children have always constituted a significant proportion of the international refugee population'. The 1951 United Nations Convention Relating to the Status of Refugees provides legitimacy and a driving force to refugee protection regimes. Although the convention is age neutral in its normative reading, in reality children are treated differently rather than as equals and the threats facing child asylum seekers are ignored or trivialized and child-specific persecution such as child abuse, child selling or child trafficking are not considered to fall within the ambit of the five 'grounds' for protection: race, religion, nationality, membership of a particular social group, and political opinion (see Bhaba, 2004, pp. 142–144). Hence children have tended to remain invisible with attention given to adult-centred issues (Sadoway, 1997). The situation of the children has been no different in the refugee crisis in Calais nor equally in the Mediterranean, garnering a global spectacle with the tragic body of Alan Kurdi being brought to shore.

Representations of the child refugee in Calais were contextualized within the symbolism of the 'Jungle' as a squalid, lawless and barbaric space. The repeated emergence of successive jungles and destructions (i.e. the first in September 2009 and the last completed on 1 November 2016) were marked by a growing awareness of the presence of children, followed by an escalation in concern about the impact of the actions (and inertia) of the authorities on children. Prior to the September 2009 demolition, there was little acknowledgement of the presence of children. The earliest mention in or around the jungle was of child refugees reduced to the animalistic, held in former 'dog kennels' that had been turned into 'makeshift cells' away from the public gaze (Perry, 2006). Prior to its demolition, the jungle was constructed as a largely child-less space inhabited by adult men, violent gangs and criminals so consistent with the symbolism of a barbaric space that left no room for the vulnerable. These constructions that followed from an under-representation of children in the Jungle was at odds with UNHCR which reported in 2008 that as many as 1609 lone refugee children had appeared before the Prosecutor of Calais and with the eye-witness accounts of aid groups and volunteers who had noted prior to the demolition of the jungle that unaccompanied children were becoming quite commonplace (Campbell, 2009; Mougne, 2010). In contrast, media represented children in the jungle through silence and reductionist accounts of their struggles in Calais. The silence as to their presence made it relatively unproblematic to legitimize the violent demolition of the camp through constructions of rooting out people traffickers, smugglers and criminals (see Howarth and Ibrahim, 2012).

The destruction of the Jungle that took place in September 2009 in the full glare of media publicity signified a turning point in the representations of children in the camps. Not only did the riot police, flamethrowers and bulldozers strip away vegetation and makeshift shelters, they also stripped away their hiding places to reveal that 132 (or half of those left behind in the camp) were children (Garnham, 2009).[3] The revelation of children and their vulnerability challenged the dominant media representations of the inhabitants of the camp as hardened young men and criminals. After the demolition, media representations of the informal camps of Calais began to fracture from these dominant representations with emerging concern for the children and the appropriate response to them in some media.

These demolitions and the appearance of the children in the camps started to shed a degree of concern over their vulnerability and the risks they faced from traffickers. With each demolition, large numbers of children disappeared. When the rest of Jungle 2 was demolished in October 2016, 1500 boys were left in a 'Lord of the Flies' scenario 'unsupervised, sleeping in bare containers and free to roam the adjacent camp site, close to heavy machinery being used to dismantle and remove the wreckage'

(England, 2016; Broomfield, 2017). Those displaced after the demolition found living conditions in Paris akin to the animalistic in environments as bad as the jungle.

By 2014, there were increasing representations of the suffering child at risk through a proliferation of images and eyewitness accounts of children taking extraordinary risks to escape the Jungle in their bid to enter Britain. Children in the Jungle included babies carried by desperate mothers across thousands of miles, young families with toddlers and unaccompanied children of 10 to 18 who had fled war, poverty and oppression (Lichfield, 2015). In early 2014, the French authorities opened a centre with accommodation where women and children could shelter at night behind locked gates protected from the violence of the camp. Images of second-hand children's toys outside the front of the shelter gave the impression of normality but the shelter itself was a symbol of the belated recognition by the authorities of vulnerability and the need to protect women and children from the violence of the camp (Ellicott, 2014). The enhanced visibility of children also came through unfolding events. As mentioned, a ferry workers strike in June 2015 led to major traffic jams around the port and Channel Tunnel and a proliferation of opportunities for refugees to stow aboard stationary vehicles in full sight of British holiday-makers. User-generated content posted on *Twitter* and *Facebook* constructed the ordinary person as a witness to extraordinary developments in Calais and the desperate measures refugees were willing to take to escape the camp. The strike had ended by July 2015, but journalists became fascinated by life in the camp and a series of photo-essays on the everyday rituals of the inhabitants of the Jungle positioned children within routine activities of washing, playing or attending to religious services (Cox, 2015; Newton, 2015).

Juxtaposed against the normalization of life in the camp were signs of the extraordinary risks child refugees faced. In September 2015 the graphic image of Alan Kurdi's dead body washed up on a Turkish beach galvanized a European public previously hostile or indifferent to developments in Calais. The image was a contested one, on the one hand it symbolized the indifference of the West to the suffering of children and on the other, it was representative of some of the enormous risks the 'migrants were taking with their children attesting to their irresponsibility'. Links to the child refugees of Calais were made through these resonant constructions of risks. In terms of resonant imagery, the grave of a child refugee in the Calais cemetery became a symbol of the suffering of children along with that of Kurdi as the ultimate price paid for the inaction of adults (Hill, 2015).

The representations of the suffering child in Calais emerged out of this context of increased visibility and contested morality on the obligations to act and notions of responsibilities of Western European nations to the humanitarian crisis. Suffering was constructed indexically in accounts of the wars, persecution and oppression in the children's countries of origin from which they fled, as well as in images of child labour and in the scars on the body of a child burnt by people traffickers (Akbar, 2015). Doctors also constructed the journeys to Calais as physically arduous and emotionally fraught, only to arrive at the Jungle traumatized by their experience in encountering the violence of the camp (Daynes, 2015). Brutality came not only from the rival gangs and people traffickers but also from the police. There were accounts of children being hit with police batons, tear gas sprayed into their eyes or having shoes removed to force them to walk back to the camp barefoot. This humiliating tactic was intended to discourage them from trying to cross the border (Gentleman, 2015).

Not only were the interactions brutal, the children suffered worsening living conditions. For most of 2014 and 2015, personal hygiene and safety were minimal, with barely any sanitation or lighting, too few water points for the number of refugees and few opportunities to shower. There was only one meal a day, not enough blankets for those in need and not enough space in the shelter erected by the authorities for the number of children in the camp. Children as young as eight or ten were reduced to sheltering in ditches or crouching in tents amidst excrement, filth and rubbish (Daynes, 2015). Doctors reported that lice, diarrhoea and scabies were prevalent and there were signs of physical and psychological trauma incurred from the country of origin, journey and experiences in the Jungle. UNHCR labelled the conditions in Calais as worse than in Turkey, which was receiving thousands of refugees every day, and an 'indictment on society' (Taylor, 2015). Refugees in the Jungle, hampered from moving on by the police and border forces, became increasingly desperate to escape the camp before winter and aid workers reported they were taking ever greater risks while tired and hungry or trusting to people smugglers and traffickers in the absence of anyone else.

Calais was the 'final frontier' (Franklin, 2014), the last border before Britain and attempts to cross it drew attention to the precariousness of children's lives. The child's life was constructed in part as being put at risk not only by the inaction of governments, but also by irresponsible parents. Newspapers claimed that 'desperate mothers drag' their babies across 5000 miles to find husbands who had already crossed to Britain (Ellicott, 2014; Robinson, 2015). Mothers were reported as hanging their babies or toddlers in a sling under a coat while they tried to board stationary lorries or slow-moving trains. Images showed a little girl being dangled over a barbed wire fence by her father or being pushed under the fence by siblings, toddlers held by the hand while they walked with parents alongside live railway tracks and a young boy being pushed into a narrow space behind the cab of a lorry by his older brother. As the signs of suffering escalated both in volume and visibility, there were calls for the government to allow some of the children of Calais to enter Britain through legal means. Cameron refused but his government did instigate a scheme to take children from the refugee camps outside the borders of the EU.

In August 2015, the British Jewish community in an open letter to the PM criticized political discourses of a 'swarm of people' and 'marauding migrants' to describe those seeking refugee as it 'morphs them into pirates, pillaging lands as they go' (Janner-Klausner, 2015). Instead they called for the refugees of Calais to be seen 'as human beings, whose needs we try to understand, rather than a problem we can solve with barbed wire'. The letter lobbied for humanity in face of this human tragedy, asserting that 'For Jewish people the sight of the Calais "jungle" camp on our doorstep is especially painful. When we look across the English Channel, we see ourselves.' The open letter made comparisons to the Kindertransport-type response during the war and pressure for such a scheme grew in support of the so-called 'Dubs Amendment' to the Immigration Bill going through parliament that would allow an unspecified number of child refugees with no family ties here into Britain. The first children were transferred from Calais under the Dubs Amendment in October 2016 before the final demolition of the camp commenced and it was closed in the first half of 2017.

In September 2016, a year after Kurdi's image had shocked the world, Amnesty International argued that the 'public outcry should have marked a political turning point, but the global response to the refugee crisis since Alan's death has been an utter disaster' (Jones, 2016). With renewed attention paid to child refugees and unaccompanied children, media discourses started to fragment, with more scrutiny afforded to their plight and the extreme risk they were exposed to. Even the *Daily Mail* spoke of the 'lost boys of Calais', reflecting the turning of public opinion since the death of Alan Kurdi and *The Times* a 'moral case' for taking children 'stranded' in Europe (Reid, 2016). Children became entities for concern in their own right and it was seen as a violation of their human rights to leave them in intolerable conditions in the jungle, and under Article 8 of the Human Rights Act they had the right to be reunited with family in Britain. There was also increasing pressure on the government to reflect and exercise their moral obligations.

The discourse of the missing children became a resonant element of the humanitarian crises in Europe. Many of the child refugees that were brought to the UK had 'disappeared' and may have been 'drawn into prostitution and modern slavery' (Hamilton, 2016). This was not unique to the UK as thousands had gone missing 'on the EU's watch', which meant that Europe had failed the children who fled war and conflict (Lamb, 2017). An independent study in 2017 found that the 'zero-tolerance policy' in Calais had encouraged 'endemic and routine' police brutality against displaced people but particularly unaccompanied children as part of attempts to deter them returning to Calais (Bulman, 2017b).

The suffering narratives of the child refugee did not entirely mitigate the hostile responses to the UK's obligations to provide refuge for these children. Those granted safe passage under the Dubs Amendment or Dublin Regulations (because they had close family in Britain) were reconstituted as suspect figures (Beckford, 2016; Perring, 2016; Wright and Drury, 2016). The first to arrive were met with a blaze of media publicity. With their faces splashed across the media, some news outlets almost immediately on their arrival speculated whether these 'man-child' figures really were children. There was a proliferation of news reports about adults lying about their age so that they could enter and newspapers such as the *Daily Mail* used face recognition software, designed by Microsoft for 'fun', to verify whether those brought in from the Jungle really were children. The 'lax' rules of the Home Office were blamed for letting in young men instead of children in need of sanctuary and there were fears for the safety of foster carers and other children in the schools where the 'man-child' had been placed.

Not only had the suspect 'man-child' stolen the identity and place of the vulnerable child in the jungle but also traded on British hospitality and humanitarianism aimed at those in need of sanctuary. Outraged at the perceived duplicity, some Tory MPs mooted the use of dental checks to verify age claims, a suggestion condemned by Labour, aid groups and medical bodies. The British Dental Association denounced the proposal, arguing not only that X-rays were an inaccurate mechanism to ascertain age but that it was also 'inappropriate and unethical' to use them when there is no health benefit (Bloom, 2016). While the government ruled out the use of dental checks, the furore created a pretext in which ministers could tighten the age criteria to 12 or under and to those that faced a high risk of sexual abuse, were Syrian or Sudanese and aged 15 or less. Lord Dubs, the British Labour politician, predicted that the new regulations would restrict or halt the transfer of children and accused ministers of breaking their promise to the children of Calais (McGuinness, 2016).

The evolution of child rights in the Western imaginary

In the social imaginary of contemporary Western societies, the figure of the child emerges through a distinctive vulnerability and a primary moral obligation on adults to protect them as vulnerable entities. The precept is mythologized in the popular premise that in the event of a sinking ship, children should be among the first to be helped into the lifeboats or saved. However, child rights are a relatively recent development in Western thought. Human rights were debated as early as the seventeenth century but children were not distinguished from adults and debates about distinctive child rights only emerged in the nineteenth and twentieth centuries (Children's Rights in Wales, n.d.). Victorian debates about child rights emerged out of imaginaries of distinctive vulnerability constructed in the recurring symbolism of the 'lost child' and popularized in the classic literature of Rudyard Kipling, Charles Dickens and William Blake, and in the twentieth century most notably in works such as *Lord of the Flies* and *Empire of the Sun*.

There are various symbolic readings of the 'lone child' that accrue in the western social imaginary. In the trajectory of popular representations the figure of the child recedes into the background as hidden, present yet unseen by society even when basic needs for food, warmth and shelter are ignored. The suffering of the forgotten child arises from being unnoticed and hence is rendered into a sense of omission or neglect. Representations of the suffering child at risk are associated with irresponsible or cruel parents or guardians whose actions betray the child or endanger their life, quality of life or well-being and expose them to violence and exploitation (labour or sexual), both witnessed and hidden. The loss is in trust; innocence and childhood are ingrained as forms of loss yet intrinsic to coming into the world of harsh realities and as part of maturing into an adult. Another set of representations of the lost child epitomized in Blake's 'Songs of Innocence' is that of abandonment; the loss of protection afforded by family life and the lone child being vulnerable to the unscrupulous and predatory adult. William Golding offers a variant of this in *Lord of the Flies*, evoked in a news report of Calais (England, 2016), that explores the acute vulnerability of children when the rules of society are dissolved and there is a descent into anarchy. Traditional values and norms around trust, life and death dissipate into lawlessness and the child is cast adrift, at the mercy of the 'horrors' that await her when adults lose their humanity.

These cultural understandings of the lost child surfaced in shifting media representations of the jungles of Calais, most notably after 2015, partly disrupting a wider anti-immigration stance encapsulated in the British vote to exit the EU. While key elements in the media supported government resistance to accepting refugees already in the EU, the child became the exception across all the national newspapers. They conjoined with aid groups to appeal to the British government to make an 'offer of hope to a lost generation', evoking a social imaginary of a humanitarian response to the suffering child manifest in Save the Children set up in 1919 to help children in post-First World War Germany, starving as a result of the British war blockade. It equally evoked memories and experiences of the Kindertransport that in 1938 and 1939 had brought 10,000 mainly Jewish children to Britain from Nazi Germany (see Janner-Klausner, 2015; Figure 5.1).

The social imaginary of Britain as humanitarian through initiatives such as Kindertransport and Save the Children have come under critical review. The Kindertransport was not a British state programme as popularly assumed but organized by private, philanthropic and religious individuals and organizations in Britain's Jewish and Quaker communities. After intense lobbying, Neville Chamberlain's government temporarily waivered immigration visa requirements for a limited number of unaccompanied children but the organizations had to fund the operation, and find sponsors and homes for the children. The rescue stopped when money ran out and the war broke out. Accounts of the Kindertransport in media and political discourse are often written in a 'self-congratulatory narrative which emphasizes British humanitarian traditions and offers a heroic tale of derring-do on the eve of war' and the fact that Britain was

Figure 5.1 The Kindertransport memorial, by Frank Meisler, which stands outside Liverpool Street Station

the only country to adopt such measures in the aftermath of Kristallnacht adds to the mythologized image of Britain 'standing alone' against the evil of Nazism (Sharples, 2012). More critical work has challenged this romanticizing of Britain's response to the Holocaust which glosses over the ways in which Jews were obstructed from seeking refuge, turned away or sent back to Germany in the knowledge they faced the concentration camps, as well as problems inherent in the programme including abuse and exploitation (London, 2003; Reinisch, 2015; Sharples, 2012). In 2015 and 2016, the mythology of the Kindertransport became a central plank of a campaign to rescue lone children from the Jungles of Calais (see Janner-Klausner, 2015).

The other mythology evoked during the crisis was of 'British traditions of humanitarianism', in particular the work of Save the Children which in 1919 and 1921 raised money to feed starving and destitute children in Germany and Russia respectively (Borger, 2015; *The Times*, 2016). British experts were also heavily involved in drafting various international treaties on human rights including the precursors the 1990 UN Convention on the Rights of the Child (UNCRC),[4] which imposes a moral obligation on signatories to protect children and ensure the primacy of the best interests of the child when considering policies that affect them.

The imaginary of Britain as a champion of child rights, particularly those of refugees, is at odds with the actions of successive governments. Britain ratified the UNCRC in 1991 but Labour and Conservative governments have resisted pressure to incorporate the Convention into UK law, arguing that it is aspirational, and declined to incorporate the rights of complaint to the UN into British law (Joint Committee on Human Rights, 2015). Instead, they have relied on a broad commitment to 'have regard to' the rights articulated in the Convention when legislating. The exception is the Welsh Assembly which has incorporated it into law, but apart from that the Convention itself does not have statutory power in the UK unless the provision falls under other legislation (e.g. for local authorities to care for child asylum seekers). Furthermore, at the time of ratification Britain included a reservation that exempted decisions on children subject to immigration control from the Convention. The reservation was lifted in 2008 after which the Government 'accepted that all children, irrespective of their immigration status, must enjoy all the rights and protections of the UNCRC without discrimination' (Joint Committee on Human Rights 2015, p. 7). In 2010, after criticism from NGOs and parliamentary committees on human rights, the government committed itself to give due regard to the Convention when making new law, particularly involving the rights of migrant children, especially unaccompanied ones.

The other key international agreement is the EU framework for the Dublin 3 Regulation of 2013[5] which places obligations on member states to take responsibility for asylum seekers who arrive in their country, but this has been largely ignored in the current crisis and refugees have had to go from one EU state to another to find one that would help them. The Dublin Agreement incorporates the UNCRC provisions on the primacy of best interests of the child, the importance of family life and a binding responsibility on the government to enable an unaccompanied minor to join a relative in a member state (cf. clauses 13–16). An Immigration Tribunal in January 2016 overruled Britain's refusal to allow four Syrian refugees, three of whom were children, to leave the Jungle and join relatives in Britain while their applications for asylum were processed. The ruling was overturned but the children were allowed to stay while their asylum applications were being heard.

There are three British laws implicated in child refugee rights and these include Children Acts 1989 and 2004, which sought to empower children, giving them a previously 'unheard voice as victims' (Davidson, 2008) and placing a statutory obligation on local councils to care for under-18s who arrive in their area from abroad seeking protection. Nevertheless, austerity policies and cuts to council funding have meant that councils are struggling to deal with the large numbers of unaccompanied children entering the county and seeking asylum.[6] The third Act is the Dubs Amendment to the 2016 Immigration Act which made provision for an unspecified number of unaccompanied children already in the EU to be transferred to the UK where their claims for asylum would be heard. Parliamentary scrutiny found that notwithstanding the lifting of Britain's immigration reservation in UNCRC in 2008, the continued oversight by the Home Office has meant that the rights and protections of child asylum seekers and refugees are subordinated to immigration imperatives (Joint Committee on Human Rights. 2015). The added complication is the protections afforded by British law protect the rights of children already in the UK, but those outside its borders in the jungles of Calais fall under French jurisdiction. Nowhere were the consequences of these two complications more evident than in the closing of the Dubs Scheme. In February 2017, the government announced that the number to be relocated under the Dubs Amendment would be capped at 350. There was an outcry, and two months later the decision was reversed with ministers blaming an 'administrative error' for not taking up offers from councils to resettle a further 130 children (McGuinness, 2017).

Contextualizing the contemporary crisis in Calais and Britain

Of the 1 million refugees who entered the EU in 2015, 96,000 were unaccompanied minors that applied for asylum in Europe in the same year, prompting UNICEF to call the contemporary crisis a 'Europe's child refugee crisis' (Rietig, 2015; UNICEF, 2016). In 2016, Europol reported that

10,000 unaccompanied children who had entered the EU were missing. These missing children were 'feared to have fallen prey to traffickers' and a year later reports suggested that human trafficking had become 'just as profitable as the drugs trade' (Bulman, 2017c; McVeigh, 2016). According to the National Crime Agency the number of children trafficked for labour or sexual exploitation had increased by 45 per cent to 982 in 2015 and Barnado's reported that the youngest child in its care of 200 in 2016 was aged 5; the majority had arrived unaccompanied and many from the camp in Calais.

The overwhelming numbers of child refugees have strained services in receiving countries, and public opinion in some European cities has 'turned hostile towards child migrants citing fears of criminality and abuse of benefits' (Rietig, 2015). These adverse public opinions and lack of empathy have drawn criticism from different quarters. Pope Francis in 2013 condemned this as 'globalization of indifference', adding that 'we have become used to the suffering of others. It doesn't affect us. It doesn't interest us. It's not our business' and two years later he argued that 'progress in civilization should not just be measured in technological advancements but also the ability to "protect life during the most fragile states"' (cf. Hooper, 2013; Vogt, 2015).

In 2017, Amnesty accused the UK of 'shirking its responsibilities' and an 'appalling lack of leadership' and warned that 'history will judge us for it' after it accepted only a few dozen separated children in the international refugee crisis (Bulman, 2017a). The organization's annual report was particularly critical of 'toxic narratives of blame, fear and scapegoating by those in power'. Amnesty argued that the 'toxic rhetoric' employed around the world 'risks taking us into a dark age of human rights and could lead to profound consequences for all of us'. The report also ascribed the risk of 'hate crime' as a factor in failure to respond to the refugee crisis, leading a to 'hateful, divisive and dehumanizing rhetoric' developing in the West, 'unleashing the darkest instincts of human nature'.

The harsh conditions awaiting child refugees in Calais were confirmed by a Lille court where 'large numbers of separated children are living' in squalid conditions with inadequate access to water and toilets and the lack of refuse collection operations. They concluded that 'this is a serious and manifestly unlawful breach of their right not to be subjected to inhuman and degrading treatment' (ILPA cf. p. 3, House of Lords European Union Committee, 2016).

In 2012, the committee reported that 1200 unaccompanied minors had sought asylum in the UK and about 2150 were being cared for in local authorities. The report called for the 'best interests' of the child to be central to asylum processes but highlighted that 'too often' immigration concerns were prioritized (p. 3) and children's best interests were considered 'only as a part of a pro forma exercise, rather than in substantive determination'

(p. 12). An earlier report also stated that although the government gave a commitment to give due regard to UNCRC when developing law and policy in 2010, it had lost momentum (Joint Committee on Human Rights, 2015). A parliamentary committee investigation into unaccompanied minors in the EU found that 'children were in crisis' (House of Lords European Union Committee, 2016) and were often confronted with a 'a culture of disbelief' and 'suspicion' (pp. 15, 21, 23) over their age and their vulnerability, imposing a tacit presumption was that they were 'someone else's problem'. This dismissive stance meant they were subjected to 'deplorable conditions', cast into a state of limbo and faced with the prospect of being returned to their country of origin on reaching adulthood, or assessed through their state of vulnerability. Witnesses told the committee of unaccompanied children being 'batted from pillar to post', and that states were 'too willing to leave unaccompanied children to pass through their territory without providing care or support', which entailed the possibility of harm to their lives as they moved across Europe without anyone taking responsibility for them (Jo Wilding cf. House of Lords European Union Committee, 2016, p. 24). Camps in Calais and Dunkirk were cited as 'stark examples of wholly inadequate living conditions' for unaccompanied children (Julie Ward cf. House of Lords European Union Committee, 2016, p. 43).

Conclusion

The figure of the child is a conflicted one. Rendered invisible before 2006 and resurrected through demolition and destruction it becomes a by-product of border politics to be invoked differentially as a political figure at varying points in time. With the capsizing boats and the pitiful lifeless body of Alan Kurdi with his shoes intact carried ashore haunted humanity as one of our deepest failings. The moral failings of the UK government in not being more receptive to child refugee resurgence in discourses of charity organizations and human rights committees and reports are again submerged in the harsh austerity politics of the Conservative government. When there are concessions made by the government to admit child refugees and unaccompanied children into the UK, these admitted entities are seized upon as suspect figures who will defraud the UK and its coffers, bringing new waves of crime into schools and onto the streets. The unhinging of the child from the status as a child becomes an important device in the public sphere to deny the child both refuge and security, and in effect humanity.

Notes

1 Named after the proposer of the amendment, Lord Dubs, who had been rescued from Nazi Germany through the Kindertransport scheme, the clause initially

required the government to relocate to Britain and support 3000 unaccompanied children in Europe but after it was blocked in the House of Commons the wording was diluted to an unspecified number determined at the discretion of the government. Rather than face a defeat in the House of Commons, the government allowed the revised clause to go through as section 67 of the Immigration Act.

2 Additional international treaties include the UN Declaration on the Promotion among You of the Ideals of Peace, Mutual Respect and Understanding between Peoples in 1965; the UN Convention on the Rights of the Child in 1989 (UNCRC); and the UN Declaration on the Survival, Protection and Development of Children in 1990 (cf. Bell, 2008, p. 10). Additionally, the Council of Europe adopted the European Convention on the Exercise of Children's Rights in 1996.

3 The inhabitants of the camp had grown from an estimated 500 in 2008 to 800 in 2009 but the able-bodied fled the camp before its demolition leaving mainly children, the infirm and ill and pregnant women behind to face the bulldozers.

4 These include the 1924 Geneva Declaration on the Rights of the child which was based on a document drafted by the founder of Save the Children, Eglantyne Jebb. The UNCRC defines children as 'every human being below the age of eighteen years unless under the law applicable to the child, majority is attained earlier' (Art. 1). In addition, Article 19 asserts the primary of the best interests of the child and sets out the expectation that signatories will protection children from 'all forms' of violence, abuse and neglect. Other provisions in the UNCRC oblige signatories to ensure the child has an adequate standard of living (Art. 27); will not separate children from their parents against their will and and will facilitate family reunification (Art. 10). There is also the obligation to provide care for those 'deprived' of a family environment (Art. 20) and rehabilitate child victims (Art. 39). The UNCRC also makes explicit provision for governments to provide 'appropriate' protection and assistance to refugee children or those that seek refuge so that they can enjoy their rights under the Convention.

5 Regulation (EU) No 604/2013.

6 Town halls estimate it costs £50,000 every year per child to cover schooling, foster care, housing etc. for child refugees. Kent County Council receives most applications and in January 2016, it had 980 child asylum seekers in its care, up from 630 at the start of August.

References

Akbar, J. (2015) 'Torture, sexual slavery and state-sponsored murder: Victims of Eritrean despot risking their lives to flee to Europe in record numbers reveal the horror of living in African state "as bad as North Korea"'. *Mail Online*, 04 November. Accessed 30 November 2016 at: www.dailymail.co.uk/news/article-3116842/Torture-sexual-slavery-state-sponsored-murder-Victims-Eritrean-despot-risking-.

Ayotte, W. and Williamson, L. (2000) 'Separated children in the UK: An overview of the current situation'. London: Save the Children.

Beckford, M. (2017) 'Those man–child migrants. Some were as old as 29: Social workers discover hundreds of adult asylum seekers have lied about their age in order to enter as "teenagers"'. *Mail on Sunday*, 01 January. Accessed at:

www.dailymail.co.uk/news/article-4078702/Those-man-child-migrants-old-29-Hundreds-adult-asylum-seekers-lied-age-order-enter-Britain.html.

Bell, N. (2008) 'Ethics in child research: Rights, reason and responsibilities'. *Children's Geographies*, 6(1), pp. 7–20.

Bhabha, J. (2004) 'Seeking asylum alone: Treatment of separated and trafficked children in need of refugee protection'. *International Migration*, 42(1), pp. 141–148.

Bloom, D. (2016) 'Dentists slam Tory MP for demanding migrants face dental checks and X-rays to prove they're children'. *Mirror.co.uk*, 19 October. Accessed 30 November 2016 at: www.mirror.co.uk/news/uk-news/dentists-slam-tory-mp-demanding-9076076.

Borger, J. (2015) 'David Miliband: Failure to take in refugees an abandonment of UK's humanitarian traditions'. *The Guardian*, 14 April. Accessed 30 November 2017 at: www.theguardian.com/world/2015/sep/02/david-miliband-refugees-uk-humanitarian-traditions.

Broomfield, M. (2017) 'Trail of misery: Following child refugees through the streets of Paris'. *The Independent*, 14 April. Accessed 30 November 2016 at: www.independent.co.uk/news/world/europe/child-refugees-paris-migrant-crisis-europe-a7684116.html.

Bulman, M. (2017a) 'Amnesty condemns the UK's "appalling lack of leadership" in refugee crisis'. *The Independent*. 22 September. Accessed 30 November 2016 at: www.independent.co.uk/news/world/europe/refugee-crisis-amnesty-uk-theresa-may-leadership-criticism-human-rights-a7592046.html.

Bulman, M. (2017b) '"Endemic police brutality": the appalling treatment of refugees in northern France'. *The Independent*, 24 April. Accessed 30 November 2016 at. www.independent.co.uk/news/world/europe/refugees-calais-northern-france-police-brutality-daily-basis-unaccompanied-minors-children-a7696076.html.

Bulman, M. (2017c) 'Hundreds of refugees unaccounted for after fire destroys Dunkirk camp'. *The Independent*, 11 April. Accessed 30 November 2016 at: www.independent.co.uk/news/world/europe/dunkirk-refugees-migrants-unaccompanied-minors-camp-fire-a7678866.html.

Campbell, M. (2009) 'Children risk lives to sneak into Britain'. *The Sunday Times*, 22 March. Accessed on 30 November 2017 at: www.thesundaytimes.co.uk/sto/news/world_news/article157205.ece.

Children's Rights in Wales, United Nations Convention on the Rights of the Child. Accessed 30 November 2016 at: www.childrensrightswales.org.uk/history-of-children-rights.aspx.

Cox, H. (2015) 'Life in the Calais migrant "jungle" with Sultan from Sudan'. *Financial Times*, 27 August. Accessed 30 November 2016 at: www.ft.com/cms/s/0/d46bc7ee-468b-11e5-af2f-4d6e0e5eda22.html#slide0.

Davidson, J. (2008) *Child Sexual Abuse: Media Representations and Government Reactions*. Abingdon and New York: Routledge.

Daynes, L. (2015) 'Gangrene and razor wire: charity in Calais is no different to a disaster zone'. *The Guardian*, 05 October. Accessed 30 November 2016 at:

www.theguardian.com/voluntary-sector-network/2015/aug/06/gangrene-razor-wire-charity-calais-no-different-to-a-disaster-zone.

Ellicott, C. (2014) 'Now desperate mothers drag their BABIES 5,000 miles to squalid Calais refugee camps to find husbands who have already crossed channel into Britain'. *Daily Mail*, 23 October. Accessed 30 November 2016 at: www.dailymail.co.uk/news/article-2804580/Now-desperate-mothers-drag-BABIES-5-000-miles-squalid-Calais-refugee-camps-husbands-crossed-channel-Britain.html.

England, C. (2016) 'Calais "Jungle" like "Lord of the Flies", with 1,500 children left behind in container compound, volunteers claim'. *The Independent*, 30 October. Accessed 30 November 2016 at: www.independent.co.uk/news/the-calais-jungle-has-become-like-lord-of-the-flies-with-1500-children-left-behind-in-containers-and-a7388021.html.

Franklin, S. (2014) 'Calais: The final frontier'. *Financial Times*, 16 May. Accessed 30 November 2016 at: www.ft.com/content/a4aa5cd8-da34-11e3-920f-00144feabdc0#slide0.

Garnham, E. (2009) 'Police swoop on sprawling immigrant "jungle"'. *Express*, 22 September. Accessed 30 November 2016 at: www.express.co.uk/news/uk/129166/Police-swoop-on-sprawling-immigrant-jungle.

Gentleman, A. (2015) 'Refugee children of Calais: "I'm very homesick, I wish I could go back now"'. *The Guardian*. Accessed 30 November 2016 at: www.theguardian.com/world/2015/nov/04/refugee-children-calais-homesick-french-police.

Hamilton, F. (2016) 'Child refugees "lost to prostitution and slavery"'. *The Times*, 12 December. Accessed 30 November 2016 at: www.thetimes.co.uk/article/child-refugees-lost-to-prostitution-and-slavery-3mznqxrr0.

Hill, P. (2015) 'Sadness of the Calais Jungle as makeshift cemetery of simple wooden crosses grows'. *Sunday Mirror*, 31 October. Accessed 30 November 2016 at: www.mirror.co.uk/news/world-news/sadness-calais-jungle-makeshift-cemetery-6743061.

Hooper, J. (2013) 'Pope Francis condemns global indifference to suffering'. *The Guardian*, 08 July. Accessed 30 November 2016 at: www.theguardian.com/world/2013/jul/08/pope-francis-condemns-indifference-suffering.

House of Lords European Union Committee (2016). 'Children in crisis: Unaccompanied migrant children in the EU'. *2nd Report*. Accessed 30 November 2016 at: www.publications.parliament.uk/pa/ld201617/ldselect/ldeucom/34/34.pdf.

Howarth, A. and Ibrahim, Y. (2012) 'Threat and suffering: The liminal space of "The Jungle"', in L. Andrews and H. Roberts (eds) *Liminal Landscapes: Travel, Experience and Spaces In-between*. London: Routledge, pp. 200–216.

Janner-Klausner, L. (2015) 'When Jewish people look at Calais migrants, we see ourselves'. *The Guardian*, 01 September. Accessed 30 November 2016 at: www.theguardian.com/commentisfree/2015/aug/13/jewish-people-calais-migrants-kindertransport-children-nazis.

Joint Committee on Human Rights (2015) 'The UK's compliance with the UN Convention on the Rights of the Child'. *House of Lords and House of Commons*,

Eighth Rep(HL Paper 144, HC paper 1016). Accessed 30 November 2016 at: www.publications.parliament.uk/pa/jt201415/jtselect/jtrights/144/144.pdf.

Jones, Stephen (2016) 'Generation war child: A year after photo of drowned Aylan shocked world, desperate stories of 12 young refugees'. *Mirror.co.uk*, 01 September. Accessed 30 November 2016 at: www.mirror.co.uk/news/uk-news/aylan-kurdi-refugee-drowned-anniversary-8703442.

King, M. (1997) *A Better World for Children?: Explorations in Morality and Authority*. London and New York: Routledge.

Lamb, C. (2017) 'How Europe Has Failed Them'. *The Sunday Times*, 17 February.

Lichfield, J. (2015) 'Calais' migrant shanty town to be provided with water and electricity by French government'. *The Independent*, 06 May. Accessed 30 November 2016 at: www.independent.co.uk/news/world/europe/calais-migrant-shanty-town-to-be-provided-with-water-and-electricity-by-french-government-10335225.html.

London, L. (2003) *Whitehall and the Jews, 1933–1948: British Immigration Policy, Jewish Refugees and the Holocaust*. Cambridge: Cambridge University Press.

McGuinness, R. (2016) '"We're not doing enough for child migrants" Lord Dubs blasts Government crackdown'. *Express Online*, 17 November. Accessed 16 January 2018 at: www.express.co.uk/news/world/733423/Lord-Dubs-blasts-Government-crac.

McGuinness, T. (2017) The UK Response to the Syrian refugee crisis. House of Commons. *Briefing paper, number 06805* http://researchbriefings.parliament.uk/ResearchBriefing/Summary/SN068

McVeigh, K. (2016) 'Number of trafficked children rose 46% last year, crime agency says'. *The Guardian*, 06 May. Accessed 30 November 2016 at: www.theguardian.com/law/2016/may/06/number-trafficked-children-rose-national-crime-agency.

Mougne, C. (2010) 'Trees only move in the wind: A study of unaccompanied Afghan children in Europe'. June. Accessed 30 November 2016 at: www.unhcr.org/4c1229669.html.

Newton, J. (2015) 'Tourists' terror at Calais: Coach passengers capture shocking footage as migrants surround their vehicle and smash their way onto a lorry heading to the UK'. *Daily Mail*, 15 June. Accessed 30 November 2016 at: www.dailymail.co.uk/news/article-3124280/Tourists-terror-Calais-Coach-passengers-capture-shocking-footage-migrants-surround-vehicle-smash-way-lorry-heading-UK.html.

Perring, R. (2016) 'Secret age checks of "child" migrants carried out to keep female carers safe'. *Express Online*. 07 November. Accessed 16 January 2018 at: www.express.co.uk/news/uk/729783/Migrant-children-secret-checks-school-foster-.

Perry, A. (2006) 'Desperate women and children held in dog kennels'. 14 May. *Sunday Express*, p. 7.

Reid, S. (2016) 'The lost boys of Calais'. *Daily Mail*, 12 March. Accessed 30 November 2016 at: www.dailymail.co.uk/news/article-3488592/The-Lost-Boys-Calais-Yes-limit-migrant-numbers-human-compassion-demands-Britain-makes-one-exception-letting-lone-children-living-squalor.html.

Reinisch, J. (2015) 'History matters . . . but which one? Every refugee crisis has a context'. *History and Policy*, September. Accessed 30 November 2016 at:

www.historyandpolicy.org/policy-papers/papers/history-matters-but-which-one-every-refugee-crisis-has-a-context.

Rietig, V. (2015) 'Issue #8: A shared challenge: Europe and the United States confront significant flows of unaccompanied child migrants'. *Migration Policy Institute*, 22 June. Accessed 30 November 2016 at: www.migrationpolicy.org/article/top-10-2015-issue-8-shared-challenge-europe-and-united-states-confront-significant-flows.

Robinson, M. (2015) 'Clinging on for dear life: Astonishing photos show two migrants lying on roof of a lorry as it leaves Eurotunnel terminal in Kent – while in Calais terrified children are lifted over barbed wire fences'. *Mail Online*, 31 July. Accessed 30 November 2016 at: www.dailymail.co.uk/news/article-3180929/Another-night-chaos-Calais-Migrants-cling-roof-lorry-arrives-Kent-children-pulled.

Sadoway, G. (1997) 'Refugee children before the immigration and refugee board'. *Immigration Law Reporter*, 15(5). Accessed at: https://refuge.journals.yorku.ca/index.php/refuge/article/view/21887.

Sharples, C. (2012) 'The Kindertransport in British historical memory'. In C. Brinson, J. Buresova, R. Dickson, R. Dove, A. Grenville, A. Hammel, B. Lewkowicz, S. MacDougall, M. Malet, A. Nyburg, A. Reiter, J.M. Ritchie, J. Taylor and I. Wallace (eds) *Yearbook of the Research Centre for German and Austrian Exile Studies*. Leiden: Brill, pp. 15–27.

Taylor, M. (2015a) 'Children suffer worsening conditions in Calais's dismal Jungle 2 migrant camp'. *The Guardian*, 19 June. Accessed 30 November 2016 at: www.theguardian.com/world/2015/jun/19/children-worsening-conditions-calais-jungle-2-migrant-camp.

Taylor, M. (2015b) 'UN migration representative: Calais camp is an indictment on society'. *The Guardian*, 23 September. Accessed 30 November 2016 at: www.theguardian.com/world/2015/sep/23/un-migration-calais-jungle-camp-peter-sutherland.

The Times. (2015) 'Help for the helpless'. 06 April. Accessed 30 November at: www.thetimes.co.uk/tto/opinion/leaders/article4402857.ece.

The Times. (2016) Lost Generation; We should help Syrian war orphans. 26 January. Accessed 16 January 2018 at: www.thetimes.co.uk/tto/opinion/leaders/article 4674351.ece.

UNICEF. 'What is the UNCRC?' Accessed 30 November 2016 at: www.unicef.org.uk/what-we-do/un-convention-child-rights.

Vogt, A. (2015) 'Leaving migrants to die at sea is akin to abortion or euthanasia, says Pope Francis'. *The Telegraph*, 30 May. Accessed 30 November 2016 at: www.telegraph.co.uk/news/worldnews/the-pope/11641723/Leaving-migrants-to-die-at-sea-is-akin-to-abortion-or-euthanasia-says-Pope-Francis.html.

Wright, S. and Drury, I. (2016) 'How old are they really? Damning verdict of face recognition software on "child" migrations as town hall chief say they'll take away benefits from any who fail age tests'. *Mail Online*, 20 October. Accessed 16 January 2018 at: www.dailymail.co.uk/news/article-3853816/Verdict-face-recognition-software-child-migrants.html.

6 Calais and the politics of erasure
Demolition, flight and return

Introduction

The recurrent demolition of the Jungles and the remaking and reclaiming of the space in Calais by the displaced Other need to be contextualized against the political and social context of France and the UK. The politics of demolition can be traced back to the historical origins of these makeshift camps, particularly the opening of Sangatte in 1999 as a formal yet temporary shelter for refugees fleeing from conflict in the Balkans and Afghanistan. Europe was not fully aware it was yet to encounter its largest refugee crisis since the Second World War and in every sense was unprepared for it. The flow of refugees created a sense of heightened tensions and the fears that Al Qaeda operatives had infiltrated the refugee trails and Sangatte added to these anxieties. Between 2002 and 2015, the predominant French strategy for dealing with migrant camps in Calais was a contradictory mix of a de facto ban on semi-permanent structures that served as shelters. Beyond this the authorities largely ignored or neglected the informal camps till these became a political embarrassment, and subsequently morphed into cultural and social threats with attendant logistical issues.

These demolitions became ritualistic episodes to disperse the convergence of the inhabitants in these camps and a mechanism to assert the intolerant stance of both governments in reiterating their fears of the camps becoming quasi-permanent settlements. These demolitions would see the refugees and displaced being sent to 'reception' centres around the country. This French approach however shifted from 2014 as the number of refugees and migrants crossing the Mediterranean began to surge and the French authorities found themselves dealing with more informal camps, growing exponentially in size.

The threat and chaos associated with the jungle and their often negative depictions in the media reports meant that the camps became spaces of myth making. The de-humanizing discourses that confronted this humanitarian problem meant that the Jungle became a space of enigma, denigration and mystery amenable to a multitude of readings. Here the 'child' figure could be turned into a suspect category and the human acquire beastly attributes, and equally the camps could reduce ordered and governed spaces into squalor. The myth and the threat of the jungle meant it had to be erased periodically as a ritual to reclaim a sense of order and control over Calais. The rituals of erasure, though, became a mechanism to contain the madness unleashed by the camp and to expiate it from the visual disarray it brought to the town as a recurrent reminder of the authorities' loss of control.

The periodic demolition of the camps and the constant dispersal and removal of the displaced refugees is revelatory of the lack of a long-term resolution for the crises in Calais. The demolitions become symbolic of the desperate attempts to keep control of a burgeoning humanitarian issue and equally the lack of concerted cooperation or long-term strategies to address the recurring bottlenecks in Calais on both sides (i.e. the UK and France). In symbolic terms, these demolitions as enactments of material erasure are performed to assuage their own sense of being constantly transgressed and occupied by the 'Other' who has colonized tracts of White suburbia while causing extreme disruption to trade and commerce. The demolitions over time function as rituals to express the stance of 'intolerance' to camps and the makeshift shelters and in effect as a means to communicate the Other as a non-human entity where these acts of demolition occur alongside the depravation of basic amenities. These recurrent acts of depravation in effect reduce the humans of the Jungle to 'beasts' not deserving pity. The Jungle as a term to address the camps captures the reduction of bare life to a fate worse than that of an animal and where shelter is seen as breeding and sustaining an unwanted life form at the borders.

The demolition and erasure becomes a tool symbolic of the power of the sovereign state and their ineffectual politics in eradicating the camps. Recurring demolitions become an ongoing struggle to claim that the 'Jungles have been put to rest and the problem has been managed'. Yet demolitions as a staging of sovereignty also bring renewed scrutiny to the lack of a concerted strategy to manage forced migration and the bottleneck at Calais. As such, Calais becomes a space of extreme experimentation with the displaced humans and their levels of resilience and what ensues is a 'necropolitics' (Mbembe, 2003) where destruction, depravation and death are ascribed to the displaced other in full measure. The jungle and its attendant 'beast' are managed through a necropolitics that is pledged to a cycle of destruction, depravation and dispersal, where children are not readily rescued from this assemblage of denigration and demise.

The hard line of the French in 2016

The most seismic shift, though, came after the Paris terrorist attacks in November 2015 and the declaration of a state of emergency that afforded the police and security services exceptional powers. By late 2016, there were concerns among some commentators, socialists and civil liberty groups of an 'escalatory dynamic' in which the state of emergency had been extended four times and fears that France was in danger of 'evolving from a state of emergency aimed at fighting terrorism to a state of emergency aimed at maintaining public order' (Zaretsky, 2016) particularly in connection with refugees and migrants. In February 2017 Amnesty International warned that French human rights were at a 'tipping point' under the state of emergency (Dearden, 2017a).

Notwithstanding such concerns, the state of emergency had widespread public support in France as anti-immigrant sentiment hardened with an increase in right-wing attacks on migrants and refugees (Zaretsky, 2016; Goldhammer, 2016). In September 2016 (a month prior to the demolition of the Jungle) French farmers, truckers and Calais residents formed a day-long chain to blockade the channel port to protest increasingly violent attempts to reach the UK by some of the estimated 7000 to 9000 migrants at the camp. The French government responded with assurances that the camp would be demolished by the end of 2016. As border control in Calais become a central issue in the French presidential elections, Pas-de-Calais (which included the towns of Calais and Dunkirk) turned to the anti-migration candidate Le Pen who campaigned on an openly anti-refugee policy and the reassertion of French control over its borders. French NGOs argued that the demolition of the jungle was intended to show voters that the migrant problem in Calais had been resolved. In reality, the French authorities could not prevent the refugees from returning. In tandem, French politicians argued for renegotiating agreements with Britain over juxtaposed controls.

These shifts in the political climate in France created a distinctive context to the 2016 demolitions of the Jungle that contrasted with the earlier 2009 incursion. Within weeks of declaring that the Jungle would be cleared in late October 2016, the French government adopted a hard line of zero tolerance towards camps, legitimizing it under the premises of law and order. After the Nice attacks in July 2016, armed presence of French troops intensified the search for stowaway refugees on vehicles (Hunter, 2016).

Prior to the demolition in 2016, narratives circulated that the army had been called in to evict 'migrants' from the Jungle in anticipation of more violent protests and resistance over the planned demolition (Mansfield, 2016). On the first day of the October 2016 demolition, an executive order issued under the State of Emergency Act created a protected zone around the Jungle where access to the camps was restricted to only those authorized to enter, which included journalists and government agencies (Bulman, 2016). Lawyers, social workers and NGOs acting for refugees were denied access to the camp, with lawyers launching a court appeal to dispute the ban. They argued that it is illegal to use an emergency law to forbid legal observers access as it breached fundamental rights by denying vulnerable people legal information at an urgent time. The 2016 demolitions failed to deter refugees and migrants from returning to Calais. In response the French government embarked on a plan of denying the refugees any form of shelter or basic amenities, to communicate their zero tolerance policy and police harassment intensified (cf. Gutteridge, 2017; Sheldrick, 2017). In line with this, the Mayor declared a de facto ban on the distribution of food to refugees in Calais insisting that such gatherings posed a public order risk. While the courts subsequently overturned the ban, the measures pointed to a willingness to use umbrella powers of the state of emergency to target vulnerable refugees and migrants. Aid groups raised concerns about 'police lockdown' and increased police brutality in the region but the authorities dismissed allegations of a heavy handed approach. Nevertheless, the reports are corroborated by volunteers accounts that returnees to Calais or new arrivals were asking for sleeping bags so they could hide in the woods to avoid constant police harassment.

The politics of immigration in the UK

In the UK, issues of immigration, particularly from within the EU and newly joined member states, became critical in the 'Brexit' referendum debate of 2016. Frustration over the UK's lax immigration policies has been perceived as one of the motives behind the Brexit vote and may be seen as an attempt to further insulate the country from the pressures of the refugee or migrant crisis (*Independent*, 2017). Although Britain is relatively insulated from the current refugee crisis because of its geographical status as an island and its opt-out of EU asylum policies, there was criticism in the media that even though the Calais camp had been demolished, Britain was stepping away from a shared 'joint responsibility' with the French for the inhabitants, particularly those that wished to join close family in Britain, including children.

For the UK, Calais had become a chronic problem. As early as 2009, the camp had grown from a few dozen to between 800 and 1000. Perceived by politicians as a hub for people traffickers and a hideout for criminals on both sides of the Channel, the camps posed a constant threat of spilling over and contaminating the surrounding white suburbs and disrupting the everyday lives of legitimate residents in Calais (Howarth and Ibrahim, 2012). In 2009, the demolition of the camp was spectacularized with the world's media alerted to the date and time. In September 2009 riot police accompanied by bulldozers, flamethrowers and chain saws organized a raid at dawn. Many of the inhabitants had already fled, taking refuge in fields and sand dunes along the coast, leaving 278 inhabitants who were unable to flee including children, the infirm and sick. The evicted inhabitants were dispersed to reception centres further away but most of them including the children absconded within hours or days (see Mougne, 2010).

Immigration Minister Eric Besson declared the demolition the 'end of the law of the Jungle and of the people traffickers' (Hall, 2009) but the spectacularized demolition drew controversy and criticism with aid groups terming it as primarily ineffectual but enacted as a publicity stunt intended to appease the British public. NGOs including Amnesty International and Catholic Rescue were highly critical, pointing out that the destruction of the shelters merely scattered the camps and handed over migrants to mafia networks without resolving the issue. Martine Aubry, leader of the opposition socialists, labelled it a 'totally inhumane act that will not solve the problem' (Hall, 2009; Gammell, 2009). The violence inflicted on the inhabitants during the raid and the trauma inflicted on the children were also criticized. The futility of the demolition was evident almost immediately as new camps sprung up in Calais and all along the coast, and their numbers grew with evicted residents returning to Calais.

The recurring phenomenon of demolition and the emergence of new camps gave way to a series of smaller demolitions in 2010, 2014 and 2015. Notably, there were two earlier demolitions, in 2006 and 2008, that preceded the more dramatic demolition of 2009. In these low-key relatively unpublicized demolitions makeshift tents, buildings or parts of a camp were flattened (Finan and Allen, 2010; *The Telegraph*, 2010; Carney, 2014). There were also demolitions of smaller camps, for example the 'new jungle' in Teteghem near Dunkirk where migrants were said to have overrun the town with the camp run by people smugglers and trafficking gangs amidst mounting squalor. Another 'new' jungle in Calais was bulldozed in 2014 because it was deemed to pose a risk to public health. Most of these demolitions attracted little more than a passing media mention with few images.

With the closure of Sangatte in 2002 and the demolition of 2016, the French authorities encountered a sustained struggle to manage the ebb and flow of refugees and migrants into the coastal port. Hence their strategy lapsed into periodic demolition to assert their control and these were interspersed with episodic intervals of indifference or neglect mediated by the degree of public attention and local agitation. This mix of aggressive and passive strategies along with increased securitization and tougher policing did not provide a consistent mechanism to manage the crisis, instead it dispersed the refugees to other spaces including 'Jungle 3' in Grande-Synthe which had from 2015 begun to garner controversy over the appalling living conditions. However, the camps were much larger than in 2009 and from 2015 the French authorities increasingly adopted a tougher stance against the refugees.

The 2015 demolition of a camp near the centre of Calais marked the emergence of a new strategy called 'progressive dismantling', adopted by the authorities for larger demolitions, most notably in 2016. The 2015 variant started with the opening of the Jules Ferry day centre for 100 women and children outside the town in January to provide secure overnight accommodation with showers, the first such one since Sangatte. In April, the French authorities created a 'toleration' zone near the Jules Ferry centre when they forcibly relocated the inhabitants to it while bulldozing the town camp. The camp on the outskirts was immediately dubbed 'New Jungle' or Jungle 2 by its inhabitants, with an estimated 1000 refugees. Between May and July 2015, four smaller camps in Calais were bulldozed or dismantled because of 'public health concerns'. By July 2015, The Jungle population was an estimated 3000 as the Mediterranean migrant crisis peaked and the camp was taking on the appearance of a semi-permanent settlement as more infrastructure was installed. With the numbers growing, UNHCR called for the Calais situation to be treated as a 'civil emergency' due to the conditions in the camp (Lichfield, 2015; Westcott, 2015). By November 2015, the estimated population of the Calais Jungle had doubled to 6000.

While most of the media, public and political attention was on Jungle 2, the tighter security and tougher police action in Calais prompted significant numbers of refugees to move from Calais to smaller camps. In Teteghem, a new camp emerged but it became synonymous among local people with a key site in which French and British trafficking rings operated. Local politicians admitted French police were generally powerless to stop French and British-based smuggling rings operating in the smaller towns and camps (Dixon, 2015; Rothwell, 2015). There were reports of rings run by English mafia using British cars with British number plates. However, these smaller camps attracted less media, public and political attention so there was a sense that the authorities were effectively turning a 'blind eye' to the camps and the criminality there while making much of the high profile, politically sensitive Jungle 2.

A smaller informal camp that first emerged in 2006 in Basroch in Grande-Synthe, near Dunkirk and 40 km from Calais, as a handful of makeshift tents in a muddy field went largely unnoticed until 2015 when numbers started to swell as refugees and migrants moved out from Calais (Médecins Sans Frontières, 2016a, 2016b; Moore, 2015). By 2015, Basroch was beginning to attract the attention of journalists who dubbed it Jungle 3 because conditions were said to be worse than in Jungle 2 in Calais. The population of the Basroch camp escalated from 100 in August 2015 to 2500 including 200 children in December compared to about 3000 in Jungle 2. About 90 per cent of the inhabitants were Iraqi Kurds. From September 2015 Médecins Sans Frontières (MSF) began providing mobile clinics in the camp.

'Progressive dismantling' of Jungle 2 (2016)

Following the 2015 demolition, progressive dismantling as a deliberate strategy was adopted to obliterate these camps over time. Progressive dismantling is a euphemism for the phased relocation or eviction and demolition of very large camps. With Jungle 2, the strategy began with the clearance of shelters and the erection of converted shipping containers capable of providing temporary accommodation for 1500 inhabitants on the north-east part. Inhabitants in the southern part were threatened with forcible relocation if they did not move into the containers but the authorities had under-estimated the number of people living in that part and those unable to find a place were forced to move into the rest of the camp or to smaller ones around Calais. Demolition of the southern part of the camp was delayed while aid groups sought court action to prevent it until the future of the children in that part of the camp[1] had been secured and to obtain a stay on the destruction of the community facilities. The court ruled that the demolition of shelters could go ahead but the community spaces had to be left intact because they provided a much needed resource for refugees and vital calm meeting places (Agerholm, 2016). As the bulldozers moved in there were violent clashes between police, refugees and *No Borders* activists who threw stones, set 12 shacks on fire and about 150, some armed with iron bars, ran onto the road to block vehicles. The shelters were flattened leaving the community buildings 'deserted in a burnt out wasteland' (France 24, 2016; Wainwright, 2016; Figure 6.1).

By September 2016, work had started on 'The Great Wall of Calais' and at the same time eviction notices were served on the inhabitants of the northern part of Jungle 2. UNICEF urged the UK government to speed up the transfer of unaccompanied children before the closure of Jungle 2 (Townsend, 2016) and aid groups warned that hundreds of Calais camp children were at risk of abduction and exploitation when the Jungle was demolished. As the first 'child refugees' arrived in Britain

Figure 6.1 Calais Jungle evictions
Source: Amirah Breen 2016. © BY-SA 4.0 International licence.

the Home Secretary appealed to no avail to her French counterparts to delay demolition until the safety of the children had been secured but the authorities proceeded with the 'dismantling' of the Jungle. Inhabitants were given free suitcases to pack their belongings; those that did not leave were forcibly evicted (Walker, Weaver and Pujol-Mazzini, 2016). Again, there were violent clashes, refugees and hard-left activists staged a sit-in protest, then set light to shelters in a bid to attempt to disrupt demolition work. In the ensuring chaos aid workers rushed in to try to prevent gas canisters from catching fire to no avail as a number exploded. Aid groups said police prevented attempts to douse the flames and then sent in heavy machinery including diggers to rip apart what the fire had not destroyed and deposit the waste in giant skips. The section being cleared was lined with riot police, some carrying shields and CS gas canisters, and wearing masks.

Aerial photographs showed the Jungle 'gradually being torn to pieces', workers in the process of ripping down the camp (Robinson, 2016). At the end of October, the French authorities announced that the camp had been cleared even though about 1500 children remained in shipping containers where they had been moved but left unsupervised, sleeping in bare containers and free to roam the adjacent camp close to heavy machinery used to dismantle and remove the wreckage, or running over the burnt-out jungle. Water and food to the containers had been cut off (Broomfield, 2016; England, 2016). There were also reports that thousands of former jungle inhabitants had fled before demolition or absconded from reception centres around the country and moved to the streets of Paris. The new jungle in the capital, dubbed 'the camp of shame' was also cleared amidst violent clashes between groups of refugees and between them and the police (Chazan, 2016a; Deardon, 2017b; McGuinness, 2016).

The making, remaking and unmaking of the camps over 18 years

The 18 year history of Calais till 2017 speaks of a space that is constantly made and unmade. Never static but relentlessly impregnated by the body politic of the other, the violent mechanism to get rid of the contaminants becomes a recurrent element. These purges are material acts of erasure but, equally, symbolic of the extreme threat the refugee crisis at the border towns and coasts imposed on the psyche of the British and the French. They were spectacularized acts performed for the public. While these became ritualistic acts of erasure to eradicate the visual blight on the towns they equally demonstrated the lack of a long-term solution for the bottlenecks. The inability to arrest the inflow of the displaced would prompt the governments to take very harsh and inhumane measures legitimized under the guise of reclaiming space from the migrants and reasserting order, constructing the refugee crisis as a chronic border issue rather than a humanitarian one.

From the closure of Sangatte in 2002 on the pretext of it being a migrant magnet, the trajectory of these erasures shows the desperation of the ineffective tactics of the authorities, giving them ammunition to dismiss the humanitarian stance and to appropriate an increasingly hard line where systemic withdrawal of basic human needs such as shelter, food, water or sanitation actually reduces the desperate and dispossessed humans to animals of the Jungle. The pseudo-rational premise of the camp as a hub of criminal activity that would consume the suburbs of Calais provided the justification to raze the camps initially. However, the emergence of new camps, in particular Jungle 2 in Calais and Jungle 3 in Dunkirk, suggested a strategy of demolition was ineffective in deterring new migrants from coming to Calais; and after the demolition of these in 2016, all tented settlements in France were seen as a lure, leading the authorities to adopt a zero tolerance policy on camps or temporary shelters.

This entailed denial of basic human protection and it also meant women and children were vulnerable to harm from individuals, police brutality or ethnic gang violence. This wilful denial of basic needs and the progressive dismantling of the camps congealed into a brutal politics of depletion. Many of the children had no blankets or shoes. The compound had running water in the toilets but taps supplying the sinks in the container compound were turned off and no food was provided by the authorities. With the denial of food, water or sanitation systems some inhabitants were forced to wash in the waste water from a chemical plant (Goldhammer, 2016). The politics of neglect became more acute in the much larger Jungle 2 where hot showers were limited in the Jules Ferry secure accommodation for women and the authorities begrudgingly installed more toilets, water points and refuse collection only after a court ordered it on environmental health grounds (see Dhesi, Davies and Isakjee, 2015). Blanket bans on the provision of shelter and food restricted aid organizations and volunteers in supporting the residents, increasingly curbing their ability to assist these refugees over time. The mayor imposed a ban on gatherings in 2017, a move interpreted by aid groups as a de facto one on the distribution of food and water to refugees until successfully challenged in the courts. In a separate action, a court ordered Calais officials to remove a skip blocking the entrance to a centre with hot showers run by a Catholic charity on the grounds that it constituted a serious and manifestly unlawful interference in property rights. While the mayor agreed to remove the skip, she reiterated a pledge to 'keep migrants out of Calais at all costs' (*Express Online*, 2017).

In Calais, until the demolition in October 2016, there was a de facto ban on any semi-permanent shelter, the exception being insufficient secure accommodation for women and containerized compounds used to house refugees during the progressive dismantling of the camp; however, this led to the proliferation of makeshift shelters and in some cases their growth into new jungles. In Dunkirk, the authorities viewed the formal refugee shelters as a lesser evil than the growth of rat-infested, squalid jungles, hence the opening of Linière and the demolition of Jungle 3. The inhabitants of the jungle who made their way to Paris encountered police 'stealing' their blankets, sleeping bags and mattresses during freezing winter weather and telling them to 'get out of France' (Dearden, 2017b). Those that returned to Calais, including children, found themselves woken by police spraying tear gas in their faces, and aid groups reported that requests were for sleeping bags rather than tents so that migrants could hide in the woods (Bulman, 2017a). The approach was endorsed by some Conservative politicians in Britain who argued that the police needed to be 'taking action before the first tent is pitched' (Groves, 2017).

The camps of Calais became steadfastly associated with public health concerns. In rhetorical terms the inhabitants of the camps were often referred to, through association with disease and contamination, as a 'migrant epidemic' or 'migrant invasion', the jungles as 'disease-ridden squats' and the refugees' attempts to stowaway on passing vehicles as contaminating valuable cargo (Gutteridge, 2015; Sheldrick 2014, 2015, 2016). As such, ridding Calais of disease-ridden jungles and contaminating migrants became a key justification for demolitions. The demolition of smaller camps in the centre of Calais was justified after an outbreak of scabies in 2014 but this was dismissed by medical volunteers as a pretext; they counter-argued that demolition was reckless, counter-productive and likely to disperse rather than contain the outbreak (Doctors of the World, 2014).

In contrast, the authorities were largely indifferent to mounting environmental health issues in the Jungle identified in an independent report that found food and water was contaminated with bacteria, inhabitants lacked access to washing facilities that would enable them to clean themselves and their clothes, and that diarrhoea, respiratory problems and skin diseases were common (Isakjee, Davies and Dhesi, 2015). The authorities did little to provide basic amenities unless forced to by the courts, and notably toilets and showers came mainly from aid groups. The apparent contradiction between action and neglect on public health grounds depended on where the camp was located. For example, in the centre of town there was a risk that the inhabitants might contaminate the wider environment; therefore public health concerns became legitimate grounds for demolition. On the outskirts, there was less risk of disease spreading to town folk and Jungle 2 was largely left alone by the authorities. When unsanitary conditions became so acute that they became a source of political embarrassment and an offence to 'French sensibilities', the camps had to be obliterated (Goldhammer, 2016).

Restoring law and order: 'the barbarians are at the gates'

One of the predominant and recurring rationales provided for demolitions was the restoration of the rule of law and public order, an escalatory discourse couched in metaphors not only of a migrant epidemic but also of barbarism and war. The demolition of Jungle 1 in Sept 2009 had been legitimized as marking an end to the 'law of the jungle', a rooting out of the traffickers and criminals who had taken hold of the camp, restoring the rule of law in Calais and re-establishing the civilized order of Western suburbia. By 2013, the cause of lawlessness expanded beyond people traffickers to include British extremists and anarchists who had infiltrated the camps who, according to local politicians and police, were 'turning Calais lawless' (Allen, 2013). The discourse was reiterated by the National Front's Marine Le Pen who claimed that 'refugees were turning Calais into a lawless jungle' but, by the 2015 summer of discontent and disruption amid the ferry workers protests, anarchists were said to be 'manipulating migrants' to stage 'mass intrusions into the Channel Tunnel' and provoking violent clashes with security forces (Bremner, 2014). Ahead of the October 2016 demolition, Scotland Yard 'spotters' were sent to Calais to help French police identify anarchists who were said to be urging inhabitants to mount resistance in the face of police aggression (Chazan, 2016b).

The account of barbarism and savages was fuelled in David Cameron's account of a 'swarm' of migrants crossing the Mediterranean and Philip Hammond's reference to 'marauding migrants from Africa' (Slack, 2015) in Calais. Amidst escalating violence during the 2015 summer of discontent and disruption, there were investigations into police brutalizing of refugees and the counter-claim that British extremists and anarchists were coordinating and fomenting violence against the police, who were being depicted 'as savages' (*Express*, 2015).

The metaphor of war equally permeated discourses where 'vicious battles' and 'turf wars' were being fought between rival gangs and Calais was described as being under 'siege' by the inhabitants of the Jungle (Bracchi, 2009). During the summer of discontent in 2015 and the disruption, black-clad riot police were reframed as the 'thin blue line' of the French police being over-run in nightly battles, their defences overwhelmed and outnumbered as 'migrants storm[ed]' the Channel 'declaring 'it's England or death' (Robinson *et al.*, 2015). There were calls by some media, French politicians and British MPs for the army to be sent in but these were dismissed by other newspapers as hyperbole and sensationalism; one such newspaper argued the issue was not the refugees and migrants, there was 'no impending mass invasion; the barbarians are not at the gates . . . Nor are the inhabitants of the Calais camp a challenge that ranks with Napoleon or Hitler' (*The Times*, 2015).

As the French police began a more active and direct engagement with the refugees and migrants they were accused of using tear gas in the Jungle. The row was ignited after a new art work by Banksy painted on the wall of the French embassy in London depicting the use of teargas in the Jungle appeared in January 2016, seen as a direct comment on plans to bulldoze the Jungle.[2] French police denied tear gas had or was used to clear camps and defended their actions by proclaiming 'it's absolutely necessary to restore public order and it's never used in the camp itself' (Ellis-Petersen, 2016). Crucially, the discourse had shifted from restoring the rule of law in the demolition of Jungle 1 to that of 'public order' in the demolition of Jungle 2 within what Zaretsky (2016) calls the 'escalatory dynamic' of the state of emergency.

Violence, self-harm and madness

The camps, besides being associated with lawlessness and filth, also became encoded through violence and madness. Camps are consumed by madness due to the lack of any possible future for these inhabitants which induces extreme desperation and futility, giving way to self-harm and violence. The desperate attempts by migrants to stowaway were described as 'becoming more maniacal by the day' and, according to French politicians, the only way to 'halt the madness' is to tighten lax asylum and welfare systems that persuade thousands to use France as a 'staging post to get to the UK' (Allen, 2009a, 2009b). Like the lepers banished to spaces on the outskirts of the cities in Foucault's accounts, Jungle 2 grew out of a relocation in early 2015 of migrants and refugees from informal camps to one on the outskirts of Calais where the madness of the desperate could be more distanced from the town and contained through the camps.

On the outskirts of Calais, the French authorities could abandon the camp to its own lawlessness, with nightly gang fights and rapes of women and children and whose inhabitants felt as if they were 'dying slowly' (Gentleman, 2015). There was also a different kind of madness, a 'common delusion', reported by volunteer doctors in which inhabitants of the camp told themselves that they would not be long in the Jungle (Harvey, 2015). Abandoned by the authorities to fend for themselves, there emerged some rudimentary forms of management by volunteers, elders and community leaders but their ability to bring order or stability to the community was limited (England, 2016).

The Jungles are also seen as unleashing a 'summer migrant madness' into the surrounding town and access routes to the port and tunnel with the descent into anarchy induced by wildcat strikes of the ferry workers and the blockading of roads with burning tyres (Smith, 2015). There was 'bedlam' at the port and closure of the Channel Tunnel as refugees and migrants stormed stranded lorries (Barnett and Virtue, 2015) and as tailbacks on Operation Stack grew longer there were calls for the French government to end the madness and reach an agreement with the strikers. As chaos reigned, the mayor of Calais claimed that the situation had become 'so lawless only the army can stop the madness' (Dawar, 2015). This was a madness not of insanity alone but of disruption to what was seen as the natural or rational order of everyday routines and business activity. These incursions were a disruption of the normal and the inability of the police to contain it prompted a call from some quarters for an escalation into military action to restore reason and order.

There was also a wider madness, or absurdity of the situation where refugees could not apply for UK asylum while outside the UK but could not get to the UK without entering illegally. For some, the hysteria over Calais came in part from a fear of foreigners and xenophobia but did not entirely explain it because 'hostility to strangers is hardly a new emotion and it cannot begin to explain the panic, officialdom and popular anger we see' (Cohen, 2015). For others, 'the atmosphere of hysteria deliberately manufactured by the image of the dead child (Alan Kurdi) obstructed rational debate about border policy (McKinstry, 2016).

The repeated demolition of the Jungles did more than deny refugees and migrants shelters, it also destroyed nascent communities and spaces where volunteers could meet with refugees and migrants, monitor accounts of police abuse and provide information and support from lawyers, social workers etc. The repeated demolitions destroyed support infrastructures that had evolved since 2015 and the worst affected were the children. Particularly, in a full Jungle 2 there were community centres, mosques, churches and schools as spaces of support for the children, as well as elders, women and families, to give emotional and practical support. But demolition was about the dismantling of support with the evacuation of adults and families, the moving of 1500 children into the containerized compound and another 70 left to sleep in the blackened wreck of what remained of the jungle (England, 2016).

The aftermath

A court order ahead of the demolition of the southern part of the camp in February 2016 had temporarily saved the self-organized community spaces (the makeshift shops, restaurants and the library, school and places of worship) after a judge ruled that they provided a much needed resource for refugees living in 'extremely precarious conditions', providing vital calm meeting places for migrants and volunteer workers (Agerholm, 2016). However, it was a hollow victory when the surrounding homes were bulldozed, leaving the community buildings without a community to use them, deserted in a burnt out wasteland. It was only a temporary stay as the main row of shops, school and library were reduced to ashes and dust during the October demolition in 2016.

All that was left was a bleak emptiness of uninhabited scrubland against a backdrop of security fences reinforced with razor wire and surveillance cameras and the sterile white container. Volunteers who had worked there for some time and seen the community grow described the emptiness as a 'surreal . . . eeriness', the camp songs and chatter in the library and school that had characterized a 'vibrant' community had become a distant memory (Robinson, 2016). In January 2017, the site of the former jungle was declared a 'no-go zone' with the intention of preventing new or returning refugees and migrants from accessing the former site, the justification being that the wasteland had become unsafe and insalubrious, littered with hazardous waste from the demolished camp including rusting cans, broken glass and bits of barbed wire (McGuinness, 2017).

Notes

1 There were 445 children (out of 3455 inhabitants in the southern part of the camp), 315 of whom were unaccompanied and the youngest was 10.
2 The work depicts a young girl from the film and musical *Les Misérables* with tears in her eyes as CS gas billows towards her and for the first time Banksy's artwork was interactive. It included a stencilled QR code at the bottom of the picture and if viewers held their phone over the code it linked them to an online video of a police raid on the Jungle on 5 January 2016 (Ellis-Petersen 2016; Mullin 2016).

References

Agerholm, H. (2016) 'Calais "Jungle": Court rejects plans to demolish refugee shops set up in camp'. *The Independent*, 12 August. Accessed 30 November 2016 at: www.independent.co.uk/news/world/europe/calais-jungle-court-rejects-plans-demolish-refugee-shops-restaurants-kids-cafe-set-up-camp-a7187726.html.
Allen, P. (2009a) 'Nothing will stop us coming to Britain'. *The Express*, 03 October, p. 3.
Allen, P. (2009b) 'Would-be immigrants forced out of Calais "Jungle" set up new camps, mayor admits'. *The Telegraph*, 19 September. Accessed 30 November 2016 at: www.telegraph.co.uk/news/6210076/Would-be-immigrants-forced-out-of-Calais-Jungle-set-up-new-camps-mayor-admits.html.
Allen, P. (2013) 'British anarchists "are turning Calais lawless": Mayor claims they fuel chaos by helping migrants that target Britain'. *Mail Online*, 25 October. Accessed 30 November 2016 at: www.dailymail.co.uk/news/article-2476495/Mayor-Calais-claims-British-anarchists-fuel-chaos-helping-army-migrants-targeting-UK.html.
Allen, P. (2016) 'Just send them to England!: Paris reacts with anger to city's first migrant camp'. *Mail Online*, 10 November. Accessed 30 November 2016 at: www.dailymail.co.uk/news/article-3923042/Just-send-straight-England-instead-Paris-reacts-anger-city-s-migrant-camp-expected-draw-thousands-French-capital.html.
Allen, P. and Thompson, P. (2016) 'Young woman was gang raped by five men in the Calais Jungle as French police cleared the migrant camp'. *Mail Online*, 27 October. Accessed 30 November 2016 at: www.dailymail.co.uk/news/article-3877384/Young-woman-gang-raped-five-men-Calais-Jungle-French-police-cleared-migrant-camp.html.

Barnett, H. and Virtue, R. (2015) 'WATCH: Anarchy in Calais as truckers armed with coshes ask "why are there no police?"' *The Express*, 24 June. Accessed 30 November 2016 at: www.express.co.uk/news/world/586599/Calais-video-footage-armed-truckers-defend-lorry-migrants-police.

Bracchi, P. (2009) 'Bloody siege of Calais: The violent new breed of migrants who will let nothing stop them coming to Britain'. *MailOnline*, 25 July. Accessed 30 November 2016 at: www.dailymail.co.uk/news/article-1202009/Bloody-siege-Calais-The-violent-new-breed-migrants-let-stop-coming-Britain.html.

Bremner, C. (2014) 'Refugees turning Calais into lawless jungle, says Le Pen'. *The Times*, 25 October. Accessed at: www.thetimes.co.uk/tto/news/world/europe/article4247273.ece.

Bulman, M. (2016) 'Human rights lawyers blocked from entering Calais Jungle during demolition under State of Emergency ban'. *The Independent*, 30 October. Accessed 30 November 2016 at: www.independent.co.uk/news/world/europe/human-rights-lawyers-blocked-calais-jungle-demolition-refugees-state-emergency-french-authorities-a7386031.html.

Bulman, M. (2017) '"Endemic police brutality": The appalling treatment of refugees in northern France'. *The Independent*, 24 April. Accessed 30 November 2017 at: www.independent.co.uk/news/world/europe/refugees-calais-northern-france-police-brutality-daily-basis-unaccompanied-minors-children-a7696076.html.

Carney, H. (2014) Police dismantle migrant camps in Calais. *Financial Times*, 28 May. Accessed 30 November 2016 at: www.ft.com/cms/s/0/8a9d752c-e665-11e3-9a20-00144feabdc0.html?siteedition=uk#slide0.

Chazan, D. (2016a) 'Paris authorities begin clearing migrant camps after influx from the Calais "Jungle"'. *Telegraph.co.uk*, 31 October. Accessed 30 November 2016 at: www.telegraph.co.uk/news/2016/10/31/paris-authorities-begin-clearing-migrant-camps-after-influx-from/.

Chazan, D. (2016b) 'Scotland Yard hunt Jungle anarchists'. *Daily Telegraph*, 25 October. Accessed 30 November 2016 at: www.telegraph.co.uk/news/2016/10/24/scotland-yard-police-arrive-in-calais-amid-fears-of-british-rabb/.

Cohen, N. (2015) 'If you hate the migrants in Calais, you hate yourself'. *The Observer*, 03 August. Accessed at: www.theguardian.com/commentisfree/2015/aug/02/why-fortress-britain-doesnt-welcome-refugees.

Dawar, A. (2015) 'Bring in the troops: Calais is so lawless only the army can stop madness, says mayor'. *The Express*, 20 October. Accessed 07 November 2016 at: www.express.co.uk/news/world/613203/Bring-troops-Calais-lawless-army-stop-madness.

Dearden, L. (2017a) 'French human rights "at tipping point" as state of emergency continues, says Amnesty International'. *The Independent*, 23 February. Accessed 30 November 2016 at: www.independent.co.uk/news/world/europe/france-state-of-emergency-extended-latest-human-rights-law-isis-amnesty-international-report-a7595251.html.

Dearden, L. (2017b) '"Get out of France": Paris police tear gassing refugees and stealing blankets in freezing conditions, report reveals'. 11 February. *The Independent*, Accessed 30 November 2016 at: www.independent.co.uk/news/world/europe/refugee-crisis-paris-migrants-france-police-sleeping-bags-blankets-violence-refugee-rights-data-a7575376.html.

Dhesi, S.K., Davies, T. and Isakjee, A. (2015) 'An environmental health assessment of the new migrant camp in Calais'. *ESRC*, (September), pp. 11–12. Accessed 30 November 2016 at: www.birmingham.ac.uk/Documents/college-les/gees/research/calais-report-oct-2015.pdf.

Dixon, C. (2015) 'Outrage as BBC boss claims marauding Calais migrants are like Joseph, Mary and Jesus'. *The Express*, 15 August. Accessed at: www.express.co.uk/news/uk/598502/BBC-boss-claims-marauding-Calais-migrants-Joseph-Mary-JESUS.

Doctors of the World (2014) '"Reckless" Calais evictions a threat to public health . . .'. Accessed 30 November 2016 at: www.doctorsoftheworld.org.uk/blog/entry/reckless-calais-evictions-a-threat-to-public-health.

Ellis-Petersen, H. (2016) 'Banksy's new artwork criticises use of teargas in Calais refugee camp'. *The Guardian*, 24 January. Accessed 30 November 2016 at: www.theguardian.com/artanddesign/2016/jan/24/banksy-uses-new-artwork-to-criticise-use-of-teargas-in-calais-refugee-camp.

England, C. (2016) 'Calais "Jungle" like "Lord of the Flies", with 1,500 children left behind in container compound, volunteers claim'. *The Independent*, 30 October. Accessed 30 November 2016 at: www.independent.co.uk/news/the-calais-jungle-has-become-like-lord-of-the-flies-with-1500-children-left-behind-in-containers-and-a7388021.html.

Express (2015) 'Now French authorities blame British anarchists for migrants storming Channel Tunnel'. 05 August. Accessed 30 November 2016 at: www.express.co.uk/news/uk/596399/calais-migrants-british-anarchists-violence-gilles-debove-french-police.

Express Online (2017) 'Judge ORDERS Calais mayor to remove skip blocking migrants from entering makeshift centre'. 14 February. Accessed 30 November 2016 at: www.onlinelivenews.com/judge-orders-calais-mayor-to-remove-skip-blocking-migrants-from-entering-makeshift-centre/.

Finan, T. and Allen, P. (2010) 'Stop being so generous to migrants: French plea to Britain after Dunkirk suburb is over-run'. *MailOnline*, 19 November. Accessed 30 November 2016 at: www.dailymail.co.uk/news/article-1331013/Stop-generous-migrants-French-plea-Britain-Dunkirk-suburb-run.html?printingPage=true.

France24 (2016) 'Clashes as authorities dismantle Calais "Jungle"'. 03 March. Accessed 30 November 2017 at: www.france24.com/en/20160229-france-calais-clashes-riot-police-migrants-authorities-dismantle-part-jungle-migrant-camp.

Gammell, C. (2009) 'New "jungle" for asylum seekers springs up on outskirts of Calais'. *The Telegraph*, 24 September. Accessed 30 November 2016 at: www.telegraph.co.uk/news/uknews/law-and-order/6223339/New-jungle-for-asylum-seekers-springs-up-on-outskirts-of-Calais.html.

Gentleman, A. (2015) 'The horror of the Calais refugee camp: "We feel like we are dying slowly"'. *The Guardian*, 03 November. Accessed 30 November 2016 at: www.theguardian.com/world/2015/nov/03/refugees-horror-calais-jungle-refugee-camp-feel-like-dying-slowly.

Goldhammer, A. (2016) 'Burning down the Jungle of Calais'. *Foreign Policy*. Accessed 30 November 2017 at: http://foreignpolicy.com/2016/02/29/burning-down-the-jungle-of-calais/.

Groves, J. (2017) 'French presidential poll favourite confirms he won't axe Calais borders deal after vowing to end the system during Brexit referendum'. *Mail Online*, 22 February. Accessed 30 November 2016 at: www.dailymail.co.uk/news/article-4247534/Emmanuel-Macron-won-t-axe-Calais-borders-deal.html.

Gutteridge, N. (2015) 'Britain now dumping £1 BILLION worth of food contaminated by Calais migrants EVERY YEAR'. *The Express*, 16 July. Accessed 30 November 2016 at: www.express.co.uk/news/uk/591130/Britain-dumping-1-billion-food-Calais-migrants.

Gutteridge, N. (2017) 'French court overturns Calais mayor's ban on charities distributing food to migrants'. *Express Online*, 24 March. Accessed 30 November 2016 at: www.express.co.uk/news/world/783436/Calais-migrants-French-court-overturns-Mayor-Bouchart-refugee-food-ban.

Hall, B. (2009) 'Refugee groups attack police clearance of Calais camp'. *Financial Times*, 23 September. Accessed 30 November 2016at: www.ft.com/cms/s/0/ac3766b8-a7d9-11de-b0ee-00144feabdc0.html?siteedition=uk.

Harvey, N. (2015) 'Calais: Syrian children are living in remote, muddy ditches'. Doctors of the World (UK). 17 December 2015. Accessed at: www.doctorsoftheworld.org.uk/blog/entry/calais-syrian-children-are-living-in-remote-muddy-ditches.

Howarth, A. and Ibrahim, Y. (2012) 'Threat and suffering: The liminal space of "the Jungle"', in L. Andrews and H. Roberts (eds) *Liminal Landscapes: Travel, Experience and Spaces In-between*. London: Routledge, pp. 200–216.

Hunter, M. (2016) 'French army soldiers go into battle against illegal immigrants as gun-toting servicemen check cars on the Calais border'. *Mail Online*, 09 October. Accessed 30 November 2016 at: www.dailymail.co.uk/news/article-3829671/French-army-soldiers-battle-against-illegal-immigrants.html.

Independent (2017) 'Our responsibility for refugees should not be forgotten'. Editorial: *The Independent*, 14 January. Accessed 30 November 2016 at: www.independent.co.uk/voices/editorials/refugees-drown-mediterranean-boat-rescue-responsibility-should-not-be-forgotten-a7527671.html.

Isakjee, A., Davies, T. and Dhesi, S.K. (2015) *Independent Report into Conditions in Calais Migrant Camps Outlines Failure to Meet Recommended Standards*. Accessed 30 November 2016 at: www.birmingham.ac.uk/Documents/college-les/gees/research/calais-report-oct-2015.pdf.

Lichfield, J. (2015) 'Calais' migrant shanty town to be provided with water and electricity by French government'. *The Independent*, 06 May. Accessed 30 November 2016 at: www.independent.co.uk/news/world/europe/calais-migrant-shanty-town-to-be-provided-with-water-and-electricity-by-french-government-10335225.html.

McGuinness, R. (2016) 'New Paris "CAMP OF SHAME": Hundreds of Jungle rejects now in squalid French capital site'. *Express Online*, 14 December. Accessed 30 November 2016 at: www.express.co.uk/news/world/743443/new-paris-jungle-camp-of-shame-hundreds-of-migrants-now-in-squalid-french-capital-site.

McGuinness, R. (2017) 'Calais Jungle RETURNS: Officials say it's LAWLESS AND DANGEROUS and deem it a "NO-GO ZONE"'. *Express Online*, 19 January. Accessed 30 November 2016 at: www.express.co.uk/news/world/756356/Calais-Jungle-returns-lawless-dangerous-no-go-zone-France-refugee-camp.

McKinstry, L. (2016) 'Migrant anarchy in Calais must not be allowed to go on'. *The Express*, 25 January, p. 14.

Mansfield, K. (2016) 'BREAKING: Calais Jungle will be SHUT DOWN on Monday as army called in to evict migrants'. *Express Online*, 21 October. Accessed 30 November 2016 at: www.express.co.uk/news/world/723885/Calais-Jungle-migrant-camp-shut-down-Monday-France.

Mbembe, A. (2003) 'Necropolitics'. *Public Culture*, 15(1), pp. 11–40.

Médecins Sans Frontières (2016) 'France: Update on relocation of migrant camp in Dunkirk'. Accessed 30 November 2016 at: www.msf.org/en/article/france-update-relocation-migrant-camp-dunkirk.

Moore, S. (2015) 'Life in a refugee camp: "the cold and fear get in your bones"'. *The Guardian*, 28 November, p. 11.

Mougne, C. (2010) 'Trees only move in the wind: A study of unaccompanied Afghan children in Europe'. June. Accessed 30 November 2016 at: www.unhcr.org/4c1229669.html.

Mullin, G. (2016) 'New Banksy Les Misérables art protests over use of teargas in Calais "Jungle" camp'. *Mirror.co.uk*, 25 January. Accessed 30 November 2016 at: www.mirror.co.uk/news/uk-news/new-banksy-les-misrables-art-7239719.

Rigby, E. and Warrell, H. (2015) 'David Cameron accused of failing to get to grip with the Calais crisis'. *Financial Times*, 03 August. Accessed 30 November 2016 at: www.ft.com/cms/s/0/e7217f16-39eb-11e5-bbd1-b37bc06f590c.html#axzz3k8NoXHSd.

Robinson, J. (2016) 'Ripped to pieces: Dramatic aerial images reveal how the Calais Jungle is being torn down just weeks after the squalid camp was packed with thousands of tents and huts'. *MailOnline*, Accessed on 30 November 2016 at: www.dailymail.co.uk/news/article-3882566/Ripped-pieces-Dramatic-aerial-images-reveal-Calais-Jungle-torn-just-weeks-squalid-camp-packed-thousands-tents-huts.html.

Robinson, M., Mullin, G., and Chorley, M. *et al.* (2015) 'Calais' thin blue line: Helpless French police are over-run as hundreds more migrants storm Channel Tunnel declaring "it's England or death" – so when will Cameron finally take action?' *Mail Online*, 31 July. Accessed 30 November 2016 at: www.dailymail.co.uk/news/article-3179285/As-Cameron-preaches-abroad-slave-labour-migrants-besiege-Tunnel-join-black-economy-MPs-demand-Calais-Send-Army.html.

Rothwell, J. (2015) 'Calais businessman "arrested over migrant smuggling ring"'. *The Telegraph*, 13 August. Accessed 30 November 2016 at: www.telegraph.co.uk/news/uknews/immigration/11800053/Calais-businessman-arrested-over-migrant-smuggling-ring.html.

Sage, A. (2009) 'Police in dawn raid to clear migrants from the jungle camp'. *The Times*, 23 September. Accessed 30 November 2016 at: www.thetimes.co.uk/tto/news/world/europe/article2601008.ece.

Sheldrick, G. (2014) '"We are outnumbered 285–1": Calais police admit they cannot prevent UK migrant surge'. *The Express*. 12 August. Accessed 30 November 2016 at: www.express.co.uk/news/uk/498507/Calais-police-admit-they-are-outnumbered-by-migrants-in-Calais.

Sheldrick, G. (2016) 'CALAIS CRUNCH TALKS: Amber Rudd to discuss TODAY destroying notorious Jungle camp'. *Express Online*, 09 October. Accessed

30 November 2016 at: www.express.co.uk/news/uk/719257/Calais-Jungle-camp-destroy-Amber-Rudd.

Sheldrick, G. (2017) 'British-bound migrants "RETURNING to Calais in numbers of more than 100 a week"'. *Express Online*, 02 February. Accessed 30 November 2016 at: www.express.co.uk/news/uk/761839/British-bound-Calais-migrants-returning-jungle-camp.

Slack, J. (2015) 'The marauding migrants from Africa threaten our standard of living, says Philip Hammond'. *Mail Online*, 10 August. Accessed 30 November 2016 at: www.dailymail.co.uk/news/article-3191665/The-marauding-migrants-Africa-threaten-standard-living-says-Philip-Hammond-.

Smith, O. (2015) 'Cameron demands EU help to stop Calais crisis following another night of migrant chaos'. *The Express*, 02 August. Accessed 30 November 2016 at: www.express.co.uk/news/uk/595489/Cameron-demands-EU-help-Calais-crisis-night-migrant-chaos.

Sparks, I. (2010) 'Bulldozing of Calais Jungle immigration camp was a "publicity stunt aimed at placating the British public"'. *MailOnline*, 13 January. Accessed 30 November 2016 at: www.dailymail.co.uk/news/article-1242854/Calais-Jungle-Bulldozing-immigration-camp-publicity-stunt-aimed-placating-British-public.html?printingPage=true.

The Telegraph (2010) 'Police clear "new jungle" near Dunkirk'. 23 November. Accessed 30 November 2016 at: www.telegraph.co.uk/news/worldnews/europe/france/8154571/Police-clear-new-jungle-near-Dunkirk.html.

The Times (2015) 'Trouble across the water'. 30 July. Accessed 30 November 2016 at: www.thetimes.co.uk/tto/opinion/leaders/article4513137.ece.

Townsend, M. (2016) 'Child refugees at Calais plunged into despair by plan to close camp'. *The Observer*, 01 October. Accessed 30 November 2016 at: www.theguardian.com/world/2016/oct/01/child-refugees-despair-calais-camp-close.

Wainwright, O. (2016) 'We built this city: How the refugees of Calais became its architects'. *The Guardian*. Accessed 30 November 2016 at: www.theguardian.com/artanddesign/2016/jun/08/refugees-calais-jungle-camp-architecture-festival-barbican.

Walker, P., Weaver, M. and Pujol-Mazzini, A. (2016) 'Calais camp refugees burn shelters as demolitions resume'. *The Guardian*, 01 March. Accessed 30 November 2016 at: www.theguardian.com/world/2016/mar/01/french-riot-police-teargas-jungle-calais-camp-evictions.

Westcott, L. (2015) 'Calais migrant crisis is "civil emergency": UN'. *Newsweek*, 08 July. Accessed 30 November 2016 at: www.newsweek.com/calais-migrant-crisis-civil-emergency-un-360768.

Zaretsky, R. (2016) 'France's perpetual state of emergency'. *Foreign Policy (Blog)*. Accessed 30 November 2016 at: http://foreignpolicy.com/2016/07/16/frances-perpetual-state-of-emergency/.

Appendix

Timeline – from Sangatte to the Jungles of Calais (1999–2016)

1999–2002: The Sangatte Red Cross shelter opened and closed. An informal camp in nearby woodland was dubbed the 'Jungle' by refugees.

2008–2009: A 'new' jungle emerged near the port of Calais and became synonymous with lawlessness, degradation and laying 'siege' to Calais.

2009 (September): The jungle was demolished, new camps emerged almost immediately in Calais and along the coast.

2010 (November): Police cleared a 'new jungle' in Tetegham, near Dunkirk.

2014 (January–October): About 1200–1500 refugees lived in makeshift camps in and around Calais. The authorities demolished three informal camps because of 'public health concerns'. The first shelter for women and children opened.

2015 (January and April): The Jules Ferry centre for women and children opened outside town. The authorities created a 'toleration' zone near it and moved about 1000 inhabitants of camps in the town to what was dubbed the 'New Jungle' or Jungle 2.

2015 (April): Tighter security and tougher police action in Calais prompted significant numbers of refugees to move to the Basroch camp in Grande-Synthe (near Dunkirk), about 40 km from Calais.

2015 (May–July): The authorities demolished four camps in Calais because of 'public health concerns'.

2015 (August–December): MSF opened mobile clinics in the Basroch camp where numbers had surged from 100 (August) to 2500 including 200 children (December).

2015 (November): The French government declared a state of emergency. The population of Jungle 2 reached circa 6000, a court ordered the installation of more amenities and Save the Children called for the UK to take 3000 lone child refugees.

2016 (January): A new £20m camp built from 130 converted shipping containers opened and the authorities served notice that they would be demolishing the southern part of Jungle 2. Inhabitants refused to move into the containers, a deadline was set, and after the authorities threatened forcible eviction they relocated but there were not enough containers and numbers surged in the northern part of the camp.

2016 (January): Numbers in the Basroch camp surged, the police prevented building materials being brought into the camp, conditions deteriorated, and the camp was dubbed 'Jungle'. The Dunkirk authorities unveiled plans for a new formal refugee camp for 8000 'migrants'.

2016 (January): Eurotunnel built a series of moats around the entrance.

2016 (February–March): There were violent clashes between migrants and protestors and the police when clearance work began on the Jungle. Some shelters were set on fire and riot police responded with tear gas and water cannon. The authorities demolished shelters, a church and mosques, but the shops, restaurants, school and library were retained after a court ruled against their demolition.

2016 (July): The authorities announced that they would demolish the rest of the camp by the end of the year.

2016 (September): Local farmers, truckers and residents blockaded the port in protest at the continuation of the camp. The French president pledged to demolish it by the end of the year and a French human rights watchdog said demolition would start on 17 October but expressed 'deep concern' over the lack of provision for children. The authorities served eviction notices on the inhabitants of the northern part of Jungle 2 and handed out free suitcases. UNICEF urged the UK to hasten the transfer of children, Rudd appealed for a delay to demolition until the security of the children had been secured. She promised to speed up the transfer process but did not specify a timeframe or numbers.

2016 (beginning of October): Violent clashes erupted over the imminent dismantlement of the camp and the police used water cannon, tear gas and rubber bullets. A pro-migrant protest rally scheduled for two weeks later was banned on the grounds of a 'possible risk to public order'.

2016 (October): Evacuation began, the jungle inhabitants were dispersed to reception centres around the country and 1500 children were moved into shipping containers. There was not enough space in the containers and the children unable to find room were left to fend for themselves as demolition went ahead. Demolition work began, a violent protest erupted between police and refugees/activists. Refugees and activists staged a sit-in protest and set light to shelters and a bus. Heavy machinery was sent in to 'reduce to rubble' what remained of the camp. Work began on the wall.

2016 (end of October): New 'urban jungles' emerged in towns and cities around France. In Paris tents, a new 'jungle' had grown from 2000 to 3000 in two days after the closure of Calais.

2016 (November): Paris police cleared 4000 asylum seekers from an 'illegal camp' under a railway bridge at Stalingrad metro station.

2016 (December): A new 'camp of shame' sprung up in the centre of Paris; a new emergency shelter was built to help solve the migrant problem.

2017 (January): There was local anger and fear of a 'new urban jungle' in towns such as Toulouse where Calais inhabitants had been sent but found themselves 'abandoned' by local officials and living in 'cramped and increasingly precarious conditions'.

2017 (January–March): The state of emergency and a zero-tolerance policy on new camps marked increased violence against refugees and migrants in Calais who were returning at an estimated rate of more than 100 a week.

2017 (January–February): The women's centre at Linière, the 'biggest official camp' in France, was burnt down within weeks of opening in a suspected arson attack. Ethnic tensions and violence rose as the camp became overcrowded with former inhabitants from the Calais jungle.

2017 (March): The government ordered the 'progressive dismantling' of it. A fire, possibly started by arsonists, destroyed 80 per cent of the Linière camp and the 1500 inhabitants were left homeless.

Index